W9-AZC-679

Gifts for the Soul

To Anne & Ann —
Have faith — all
things are possible!
With Love & Light,
Dawn E. Clark.

Also by Dawn E. Clark

☀ *Tuning In: Opening Your Intuitive Channels*

☀ *Perceiving Energy: Beyond the Physical Form*

Gifts for the Soul

A Guided Journey of Discovery, Transformation and Infinite Possibilities

DAWN E. CLARK

AARRON
PUBLISHING

Gifts for the Soul

Copyright © 1999 by Dawn E. Clark

Printed and bound in the United States of America

This edition is a compilation, expansion and revision of works previously published as *Images of Soul* Copyright © 1997 by Dawn E. Clark and *Synergistic Soul Concepts* Copyright © 1998 by Dawn E. Clark.

All rights reserved. No part of this book may be reproduced by any mechanical, photographic, or electronic process, or in the form of a recording, nor may it be stored in a retrieval system, transmitted, or otherwise be copied for public or private use without written permission from the publisher. For information please address Aarron Publishing, P.O. Box 271203, Houston, TX 77277-1203.

Aarron Publishing titles may be purchased for educational, business, special sales or promotional use. For more information please write: Special Markets Department, Aarron Publishing, P.O. Box 271203, Houston, TX 77277-1203.

Important Note for the Reader

The ideas, procedures, and suggestions contained in this book are not intended to replace the services of a licensed physician, therapist, or health-care practitioner. The author, editors, and publisher cannot be held responsible for the consequences of trying the ideas, suggestions, and techniques in this book in a program of self-care or under the care of a licensed professional. The ideas, suggestions, and techniques in this book should not be used in place of sound medical therapies and recommendations.

FIRST EDITION

Library of Congress Catalog Card Number: 99-61373

ISBN: 1-928532-00-4 (HC)

ISBN: 1-928532-01-2 (PBK)

99 00 01 02 03 ❖ AP 10 9 8 7 6 5 4 3 2 1

To my Dad,

who brought many truths to light.

Acknowledgements

Infinite love and gratitude go to my dear friend Aarron Light, whose kind, ever-present support fills me with strength. Boundless love goes to my children, Clark, Katherine Elise and Christopher, who fill me with joy. Deep appreciation and love to my mother and her husband, Flora and Dietmar Graf, and to my sister and her husband, Desirée and Sam Wilson.

Special thanks and love to Kathy Elmore for her insights and grammatical wizardry. Many thanks and love go to Kirsten Coco, Dr. Francesca Russo, Nell Calaway, Patter Gersuk, Robert Boustany, Michelle Balthazar, and countless other friends, for supporting me during this writing process. I also acknowledge and thank numerous clients and readers, who provided me such rich experiences about which to write. Names have been changed to protect anonymity.

How To Contact The Author

Dr. Dawn E. Clark presents lectures, seminars and workshops for individuals, businesses, associations and non-profit organizations nationwide. For information please call or write to the address below. Readers of this book are also encouraged to contact the author with comments or experiences.

The Center for New Beginnings
P.O. Box 5485
Kingwood, TX 77325-5485

Telephone: (281) 359-5154
Fax: (281) 359-1069
e-mail: Center4NewBeginnings@juno.com

Contents

Contents

*T*his book was written in cooperation with God. By day, I was busily occupied writing a spy novel, but at night some mysterious force kept pulling me out of bed, half asleep, to sit at my computer and write this book. I frequently worked for hours at a time, with my eyes closed, typing as quickly as I could to capture the words that were channeled to me. From time to time my ego would try to add a section, a chapter, or a case study. Inevitably, I would find these additions on my disk to be unretrievable or discover that the c: drive had failed to save the last version. I was allowed no exceptions in this area. It seemed the book was to contain only that which God would have it contain.

I wrote on faith. When people asked me what the book was about, all I could answer was that it was about healing. When it was finally "finished" and the time came to edit the work, I discovered that it did indeed have a central theme and purpose. That purpose is to offer the world a new way of healing soul fragmentation and core life issues, a way devoid of mysticism and accessible to everyone. It offers this healing in a way that serves to empower people, rather than keep them dependent upon therapists, shamans or other healing practitioners.

I realized even as a child that I possessed intuitive capabilities that my playmates and family did not understand. In my counseling practice, I combined these abilities with traditional methods of psychotherapy to help my clients heal the troubling issues in their lives. While most responded quickly, a few seemed to require something more for healing to occur. I asked to be shown a better way to help them. While new modalities and techniques were unveiled which greatly increased the speed and ease of healing, each still required the assistance of a therapist or healing practitioner.

Finally, I asked to be shown a way which would enable people to heal themselves. *Gifts for the Soul* is the culmination of that prayer. As you read through the case studies, you will understand how this evolution in healing progressed from dependency on others to the ability to heal ourselves. These Gifts will enable you to heal lifetimes of lessons and physical ailments, reconnect with your higher self, and discover your intended path. Ultimately, as you follow that path, you may even choose to teach others.

Enjoy your journey . . .

THE CIRCLE OF LIFE

: Chapter 1

M y Dad died suddenly one cold January morning, and in an instant I learned what it means to grieve. We had only had two years together because of his work as an intelligence agent, and I felt cheated out of a lifetime with him. I alone was with him when he died. Mom did not have the strength to be at the hospital. Dad's constant absences from our household had left many issues between them unresolved, and a final good-bye on those terms seemed more than she could bear.

I stood at his deathbed as the last breath of air left his lungs. The heart monitor straight-lined, and suddenly I felt a warm and comforting presence by my side. The fact that I held his lifeless hand tightly in mine seemed inconsequential as the warmth of an arm enveloped my shoulders. I knew this warmth was the spirit of my father. Slowly, I allowed myself to be comforted by this gentle spirit, and just when I thought the comforting presence would stay, it disappeared. Seconds later, the cold, harsh reality of the Intensive Care Unit returned as a nurse entered and asked me to accompany her to fill out the necessary paperwork. After what seemed like hours, I finally arrived at home feeling lonely and empty.

Over the course of the next few days the same soothing energy presence appeared in my bedroom several times. This energy body, which was gold and white, brought me a great sense of calm. Shortly thereafter, the dreams began. They were far more realistic in nature than my usual dreams, and in them Dad would reassure me over and over that he was still there for me and that he was fine. He appeared as he had in life at varying ages, and though the dream visits tended to be short, they were quite intense. Usually he had some important message for me and then would leave before I had the chance to tell him how much I missed him.

A couple of weeks after Dad's death, I had a surprising early morning phone call from his best friend, Tiny. His voice was filled with fear.

"Can you come over right away?" he asked. "I need to talk to you."

When I arrived at his house, Tiny, a three hundred-pound man, appeared visibly shaken.

"I saw the strangest thing this morning," he said breathlessly. "It wasn't a dream. I know it wasn't. It was really him!"

"Okay, Tiny," I replied slowly. "Let's sit down and talk about it." Taking a deep breath, I settled into the sofa and said, "Now, tell me exactly what happened."

"Well," he responded hesitantly, "I was lying in bed this morning when I thought I saw someone standing in the doorway. I looked over and realized it was your Dad. I swear! Big as day, just standing there looking at me." He paused, glanced up at me and continued, "Dawn, he scared the crap out of me!"

He shakily lit a cigarette and then resumed his tale.

"I couldn't even utter a word. I was so scared. He came right over to me, to the side of my bed."

"Go on," I said.

Nervously, he continued, "Then your Dad just smiled at me and said, 'Tiny, you old son of a bitch, I want you to have my watch. You know, the gold Timex. We've spent a lot of time on surveillance together, and it's supposed to be yours.' I managed to croak out an 'Okay.' Your Dad just stood there for a moment and, just when I was beginning to feel comfortable, he turned and walked away. Before he got to the doorway, he looked back at me and said, 'Get it today Tiny. I'll be seeing you soon,' and then he disappeared."

He shook his head slowly in wonder for a moment before he continued.

"Dawn, I swear, he looked just like he did before he died. He was wearing his white shirt and those khaki colored pants." Tiny looked at me with eyes that pleaded for understanding. "You believe me, don't you?" he asked anxiously.

"Yes, Tiny, I believe you," I said calmly.

"I thought you'd think I was crazy," he sighed.

"No," I said, "I've seen him, too. And I can get you the watch today. Will that make you feel better?"

"That would be great," he replied. "But Dawn," he said as he took a shaky breath, "What I really want to know is what he meant by, 'I'll be seeing you soon'? Do you think he's coming back?"

As I looked into the frightened eyes of my father's friend, I knew exactly what my Dad had meant. But I couldn't bring myself to tell him. I stayed with Tiny another half hour, reassuring him that even if Dad came back to visit again, there was no need to be afraid.

As promised, I dropped the watch off at Tiny's house later that day. Two weeks later, Tiny died suddenly of a brain aneurysm while watching television. He was wearing my Dad's watch.

A NEW ASSIGNMENT

*L*ess than a year and a half after my father's death, I married a man my father had never met. Soon our plans to create our own family were underway. Dad's visits entered a new dimension after the birth of my first son, Clark. One night, just as I was drifting off to sleep, I suddenly felt a presence standing over me. I opened my eyes and was startled to find my father standing there looking down at me. I tried to speak but couldn't. He smiled and said, "I came to see my grandson." He held out his left hand, the same hand I had held as he died. Hesitantly, I reached up and took his hand as he gently helped me up out of bed. Part of me was petrified because I had never before seen his spirit materialize into such a solidly dense and recognizable form. This experience was entirely different from the way Dad had looked in dreams or as he had appeared in the gold and white energy body shortly after his death.

Still unable to speak, I walked hand in hand with him to the nursery. I quickly grew more comfortable and was elated to have my father see the child I never thought he would know. As we stood by the crib looking at the sleeping infant, I said proudly, "His name is Clark."

"I know," Dad said softly. I looked at him in surprise. He smiled at me, looked back at the sleeping baby and then disappeared. I was left standing at the crib by myself.

Over time, Dad's visits became less frequent. The final shift came about four years after Clark's birth when I was called – virtually summoned – out of my body to see him. I had never experienced this type of astral travel before. At first the sensation of my spirit being drawn out of my body was frightening, and I fought against it. Each time I would near the ceiling, I struggled to pull myself back down. Finally, I just let go and floated up higher and higher, not knowing where I was going or what I was supposed to do. I ascended for what felt like five minutes. The Earth disappeared below me and all was dark for a long time. When light finally came again it was in the form of a soft white glow, which surrounded a structure floating in the engulfing darkness.

Dad met me at the entrance, but he appeared very different from before. He did not look as he had in the lifetime when I knew him. He now appeared as an etheric, light colored energy body, whose soul I recognized the instant I looked into his eyes. He smiled at me, took me by the hand and led me inside.

20

"That is where you must walk," he said, pointing down at the eighteen inch-wide path under my feet. He, on the other hand, did not seem restricted to this footpath at all. He led me over to a counter inside this strange sort of astral café and asked if I would like a cup of hot tea.

"Yes," I replied slowly, "that sounds wonderful. How about you, Dad? Won't you have one with me?"

"Of course not," he laughed, "don't be silly."

When my tea arrived, he escorted me over to a booth where we sat down across from each other. Amazed at my surroundings, I looked around at this peculiar meeting place. Other spirits also sat at neighboring tables and booths talking with living people like myself. The structure itself seemed to have no walls but rather was encompassed by a dome-shaped energy field.

I felt Dad take my hand into his again. He looked at me intently across the table. Our eyes met and our souls connected. He looked so happy. Never in all my life had I seen such joy in his eyes. I spent a moment marveling at his appearance. He was exquisitely beautiful. It was as if I were visiting with his higher self, totally devoid of earthly form.

"I won't be able to come and see you anymore," he began in a comforting tone, "I have been given a new assignment."

I couldn't believe he still talked in spy talk.

"This is the best mission I've ever gone on," he continued, "and I can't tell you how happy it makes me."

"What is it?" I asked excitedly.

He smiled. "I can't tell you," he said, looking even more deeply into my eyes, "but you must know that I will always be with you."

"Yes," I said understandingly. "I know that." I was so happy for him that I did not even feel sad about the possibility of not seeing him anymore. Never had I seen my father filled with such joy.

Then, unexpectedly and with a sense of urgency, he said, "It's time for you to go now."

"But I haven't finished my tea yet," I protested. "Can't I stay just a little longer and visit?"

"No, you must go now," he said gently but firmly. "I have told you what I needed to tell you. Remember I will always be with you."

"Yes, Dad," I said, and just as I began to tell him I loved him, I felt myself disengage from my surroundings and begin to float downward. It was an incredibly long way down, but the descent was slow, and I felt safe the entire time. As I re-entered my body, I took a deep breath and slowly began to regain control of the vessel that held me earthbound. With great concentration and a concerted effort, I began to move first my fingers and then my feet. Soon I felt completely back in body.

The next day I excitedly shared my adventure with a close friend. As supportive as she tried to be, I think it was just beyond her realm of understanding. Days turned into weeks, and as time passed, I remained filled with joy for my father and his new mission. For the first time since his death I did not miss him.

THE MISSION

*T*ime flew by. My father had been gone seven years. When I became pregnant with my third child, my friends wondered why I would even consider having another child, as my marriage was far from perfect. Nevertheless, I felt compelled, almost obsessed, to have another baby.

The delivery was grueling. The epidural anesthesia for the C-Section failed, yet I remained insistent on being totally conscious for the birth. My doctor reluctantly agreed to deliver my son under local anesthesia, shaking his head and saying he had only done it once before in a taxicab under emergency conditions.

Painstakingly, he injected my abdomen numerous times along the length of the impending incision and then turned to me and said, "This will only numb you about one-half inch down. You will have to tell me when you feel me cutting, and I'll reinject at the next level."

Over and over I felt the searing, hot pain of the scalpel in my belly and then the blessed burning of xylocaine injections that numbed the pain. I prayed to pass out, but I didn't. As with all things, God had a plan.

A few moments later, fully lucid, I proudly held my tiny son in my arms. Looking deeply into his eyes, I was panic stricken as I watched his face transform into that of my father's. I was looking right into my father's eyes, and he was smiling at me.

Tightness shot through my chest. I was stunned! Was I losing my mind? It had never occurred to me that my father would come back as my son. My mind reeled. It couldn't be my father. "It must be shock," I kept telling myself, "or stress from the delivery." It was just not possible. Or was it?

Each time I held the child in my arms and our eyes locked, my father's image would appear. His eyes looked older than time. Slowly I grew accustomed to the transformation and became comfortable seeing my father's face appear before me as I held this tiny child in my arms. Nevertheless, it was an experience I spoke of to no one. Who else could have understood?

My mother came to visit me later that day. She sat down in the chair next to my bed and said, "Oh, let me hold him!"

Not long after I handed the tiny, sleeping baby to her, Christopher began to wake up. Looking down into his eyes, she cooed, "Oh, you are so precious. Hi, there little one."

Then, all of a sudden, her eyes grew wide and with a startled gasp, she hurriedly handed the baby back to me. Trembling, she stood up and, in a choked whisper, said, "I'm sorry, but I have to go now."

I knew what she had seen. "No, please don't go," I said quietly. "Everything is all right. Sit back down."

"No, no, I have to go," she insisted.

It took a few minutes to calm her. Finally, she reluctantly agreed to stay on the condition that she didn't have to hold the baby. After a long period of silence, she finally said in a shaky voice, "You won't believe what I saw."

Her eyes filled with tears as she stared blankly down at the floor. "When I looked into his eyes, I saw your father's face."

"I know," I said softly.

My mother looked up at me in amazement. "You've seen it, too?"

"Yes," I said. "It frightened me at first, but it's really not so bad once you get used to it." I then spoke of what I had seen and tried to reassure her. But badly shaken, she steadfastly refused to hold the baby again.

It was days later, after I was back at home, before she summoned up the courage to hold her grandson once again. At first she avoided his eyes, but then she finally looked. Gasping, she bravely continued with the soul gaze and then began to cry. She handed him back and insisted on leaving. And so it went for the first few months. Over time Mom became more accustomed to the unusual occurrences surrounding her youngest grandson and was able to support and understand Christopher.

Not wanting to be branded delusional, I shared my secret with no one else. Christopher's father, however, often commented on how Christopher's eyes seemed to change from time to time in a way that made him nervous.

My friends too would often say, "His eyes certainly look old for his age," or "What wise eyes he has!" or "He's an old soul."

Over time, the frequency of the facial transformations diminished. After about six months, all that occurred was a shift in the child's eyes whenever I connected with my father. Christopher's behavior, however, still remained a bit unusual.

At nine months of age, he would sit in the rocker watching the world news for a half an hour or spend long periods of time methodically going through reference books and novels. He had little or no interest in playing age appropriate games, and never has. When people commented on this behavior, I would simply smile and say, "I know it's a little strange, but that's just the way he is."

Yet, despite all I had seen, skepticism remained embedded deep within my heart, and I yearned for more solid proof that this little boy to whom I had given life actually embodied the soul of my father. Later events, however, would provide undeniable evidence, even to Christopher's father.

Chapter 4

By the time Christopher was a year and a half old, I was desperate for substantiation. As he was climbing into the tub one evening, I decided to ask him point blank. "Christopher," I said, "did your name used to be Jim Clark?"

He turned and looked at me with those eyes, then very seriously and matter of factly replied, "Yes," and proceeded to sit down in the tub.

The skeptic in me immediately thought, "Oh sure, he'd probably say 'yes' to anything. So I then asked, "Did your name used to be Sam Jones?"

The intensity of his reaction surprised me. He shot me an angry look, and emphatically replied, "No!"

"Okay, Okay," I thought, "I believe you," but within hours the doubt crept back in. Thankfully God is patient and kind as we go through our learning, and He continued to offer me proof.

One of my fondest memories is of an exchange Christopher and I had when he was two. As I walked out of the bedroom one morning, he turned to look at me and, in a very condescending tone, said, "That is my shirt but you *may* wear it." I was taken aback by his authoritative inflection, but looking down, I realized that I had indeed put on one of my father's old shirts that I hadn't worn in years.

I decided to call his bluff. "No," I replied, smiling in an effort to mask my surprise. "This is my shirt. I have had it a very long time."

But he was adamant. "No, it is not," he said firmly. "It is my shirt. I know it is my shirt, but you *may* wear it."

At this point, I knew I wasn't going to win this argument, so I just gave him a big hug and said, "Okay, honey, it's your shirt," and I quietly thanked God for providing more of the evidence I longed for.

A few days later, another bewildering incident occurred. The kids were sitting in the den reading while Christopher's father was watching television. Suddenly, Christopher stood up, walked over to the bookshelf and pulled down the globe. As I looked on from the kitchen, he walked over to his father, matter-of-factly pointed to a place on the globe, and in an incredibly solemn tone said, "This place is Vietnam." His father humored him, took a look at the globe, and was astounded to see that Christopher's finger pointed right at Vietnam.

"Yes," he replied with surprise.

As Christopher continued, a pensive expression flooded over his face. He moved his finger to other spots on the globe.

"And this place is Korea. And this is Germany, isn't it?"

At this point, his older brother and sister came running over. "Wow, how do you know that?" Katherine Elise, his five-year-old sister, blurted out.

"I don't know," he said with a shrug. "But this is where we live right now."

"Yes, that's right!" said Katherine Elise, looking at the tiny finger pointing to Texas. Just as she was about to engage him in further global explorations, he switched back to his two-year-old self and walked away from his siblings to seek out a toy.

I looked on from the kitchen, not saying anything, re-membering that Dad had served in all those places. This rapid transformation, from child to past life memories, still confuses his siblings today. That day they just looked at each other dumbfounded and went back to reading their books.

By this time, I had accepted that Christopher was my father's reincarnation. This acceptance continues to help me better understand him and deal with the residual past life emotions that occasionally motivate his behavior. An example of how past life experiences can seep through into the present occurred the following summer when we went to the pool to go swimming. Christopher was petrified of the water and re-peatedly refused to go in. I tried swimming lessons. I tried ig-noring his fear and letting him stay out of the water. I tried forcing him to go in. Nothing worked. Finally one day, I just asked him, "What are you afraid of?"

"The alligators," he said earnestly.

In an effort to quickly dismiss what I judged to be child-hood fantasizing, I playfully replied, "Oh, there are no alliga-tors. Come on, let's go in."

"Yes, there are Mommy! I know there are!" he insisted as he desperately clung to my leg. As I looked down at my terri-fied son, I saw my father's eyes.

At that point, I realized that I was dealing with an issue which transcended this present lifetime. His fearful belief about alligators in the swimming pool seemed so fantastic it was hard to take seriously, but my intuition told me I needed to listen. We sat down on the side of the pool for a moment. I took a deep breath and cleared my mind. Silently I asked for guidance, and just then a memory of my father flashed before me. I remembered him telling me a story about how he had learned to swim. At age six, his uncle had thrown him in the alligator infested waters of the Pearl River in Louisiana.

All of a sudden, everything made sense. Christopher's memories of his past life experience with alligators made him perceive them as a very real danger now as he began to learn to swim in this lifetime. Obviously this soul memory was still viv-idly accessible to him and was not just a childish fear to be quashed by an adult. I decided to change my approach and talk openly with him about his previous experience.

I held him gently on my lap and asked, "When you learned to swim last time there were alligators weren't there?"

He nodded, "Yes," as a silent tear rolled down his cheek.

"You were scared, weren't you?"

Choking back sobs, he said in a small, broken voice, "I was afraid they were going to eat me."

"There are no alligators this time," I assured him. "You are safe with me. I promise. It will be different this time."

Still anxious, he turned to me and asked, "No alligators? Are you sure, Mommy?"

"Yes, I am sure," I said. "Come on, I'll go with you." He placed his small hand in mine and held on very tightly as we went into the pool.

After about five minutes, he looked at me with smiling eyes and said, "You're right Mommy, no alligators."

The check for alligators continued the entire summer of his third year.

The pinnacle of proof came after Christopher's fourth birthday. I was grateful that his father witnessed this event also, or he may have never believed me. We were all sitting at the table eating dinner. Christopher was particularly somber and hadn't eaten anything on his plate.

"What's wrong?" his father asked him.

"My birthday's coming up," Christopher replied reflectively.

"You just had your birthday in October," his father said.

"No, my *real* birthday," Christopher insisted.

"Well, when is your *real* birthday?" I asked.

Looking me squarely in the eyes, he replied, "January seventh."

My mouth must have dropped open. That was certainly not the answer I had expected. Not only had my four-year-old given a date in ordinal number form, which he had never used before, but the date itself was conclusive in my mind that this little body sitting before me was in fact the new home of my father's soul. I looked at Christopher's father and quietly asked if he knew what January seventh was.

"No," he replied as he continued to eat his dinner.

"It's the date of my father's death," I said soberly.

"Well, how did he know that?"

"I don't know," I replied. "I never talk about it. You didn't even know."

We just looked across the table at each other in silence. After that, even Christopher's father could not deny the unique experiences that centered around this child. A couple of months later when January seventh finally did roll around, Christopher walked up to me in the kitchen and unexpectedly remarked, "Today is my birthday, isn't it, Mommy?"

I reached down, held him in my arms, and softly replied, "Yes, baby, it's your special day."

Perhaps Christopher believed this to be his birthday because it was the day his soul was set free from my father's tormented body, which had prematurely deteriorated due to Agent Orange exposure in Vietnam. Whatever the reason, he smiled and walked away and has never talked about it since.

Years later, Christopher still has moments when my father's memories flood into his consciousness. Once, when the family was busily planning a trip to Colorado to visit my father's brother, John, Christopher began to insist that he was not John's great nephew, but rather his brother. The children had never met John, so I asked my oldest son, Clark, to explain the family tree to Christopher. Clark patiently explained the family relationships to Christopher, going over and over the fact that John was Christopher's great uncle, not his brother. But, despite all Clark's explanations, Christopher remained entrenched in his position.

"No, Clark," he firmly replied, "you don't understand. I may be that on the outside, but on the inside, I'm John's *real* brother."

Over time, my experiences with Christopher proved to me how vital it is to validate and accept all aspects of children's personalities. Even the unusual, extraordinary, or bizarre should be honored and heard. Can we really be sure that the invisible friends some children claim to have are truly imaginary? Or are these children just very much in touch with the spirit world from which they recently came?

When we are born into a new life, we do not necessarily shut down our soul's memories of previous lives. These memories are often readily accessible and may manifest in the form of recurring dreams, unusual preferences, unexplained fears, or in the speaking of profound truths.

Perhaps you can recall a similar experience yourself. Have you ever felt like you have been in a certain place before, but you knew it wasn't in this lifetime? Maybe you have a strong fear of snakes, heights, airplanes, or alligators that you can't explain, yet chills you to your core? Could its origin exist in a past life experience? Or have you ever wondered at the patterns in your life that seem to repeat themselves over and over in your relationships, your finances, or your health? Could it be that you are reliving the mistakes of a past life in an effort to remember and heal in this lifetime?

If our own memories from past lives had been validated when we were children, perhaps we would not have so much healing to do as adults.

Our present Western culture makes it difficult for us to readily accept the concept of reincarnation, much less publicly talk about our experiences. But it wasn't always so. There was a time when the Christian Church, as well as Western philosophy, embraced the belief in reincarnation.

REINCARNATION AND THE EARLY SCRIPTURES

*H*ave you ever gazed into someone's eyes and felt an extraordinary connection with that soul? Was there ever a time when you met someone and knew beyond a shadow of a doubt that your experience with that person transcended this lifetime?

Despite the fact that these experiences are common, many people are reluctant to speak openly about them. This reluctance is generally based on a fear of what others may think. Our contemporary Western culture, our traditional religious backgrounds, and our families may offer little validation for experiences that may be explained by reincarnation. Many times, it is easier to summarily reject what we have experienced, and act as if it never happened, rather than explore the potential answers.

Yet, deep within, we often know that it is our acceptance of present Western cultural beliefs that causes us to choose to live in denial of a fact that our heart and soul know to be a truth. Belief in reincarnation does exist in Western philosophy, and it did in early Christianity as well.

Plato, in the 4th century BC, stated that, "Soul is older than body. Souls are continuously born over again into this life. Know that if you become worse, you will go to the worse souls, and if better, to the better souls; and in every succession of life and death, you will do and suffer what like must fitly suffer at the hands of like."

Origen (185-254 AD), philosopher, teacher, and influential theologian of the early Christian Church, became famous in his time for preserving original versions of the Scriptures. In *De Principiis*, he wrote: "Every soul . . . comes into this world strengthened by the victories or weakened by the defeats of its previous life. Its place in this world as a vessel appointed to honor or dishonor, is determined by its previous merits or demerits."

The early Christian saints also spoke of the soul's reincarnation as well. Saint Gregory (257-332 AD) affirmed that "it is absolutely necessary that the soul should be healed and purified, and if this does not take place during its life on earth, it must be accomplished in future lives." In the 4th century AD, Saint Jerome affirmed Origen's belief in the soul's reincarnation when he proclaimed him to be "the greatest teacher of the Church since the Apostles." Saint Augustine (354-430 AD) wrote that Plato's philosophy was "the purest and the most luminous of all philosophy . . . and that Plato was born again in

Plotinus." Plotinus (205-270 AD), a philosopher and fellow disciple of Origen, avidly acknowledged reincarnation in his work entitled *The Descent of the Soul*.

If these early Christian saints, anointed with the highest honor their Church could bestow, all held such resolute beliefs in reincarnation, then what caused the concept of reincarnation to disappear from Christian teachings? Acknowledgment of the soul's reincarnation was in fact embodied in various parts of the early Gospels prior to the sixth century. It was in 553 AD, that the Fifth Ecumenical Congress of Constantinople condemned the teachings which affirmed reincarnation.

The summoning of the Fifth Ecumenical Congress was the result of Byzantine Emperor Justinian's efforts to establish the supremacy of the Monophysite Doctrine in the Christian Church. This Doctrine not only denounced reincarnation, but also cataclysmically divided the Church into two adversarial factions over the nature of Christ.

To ensure support for the adoption of his Doctrine, Justinian permitted only six Western bishops to attend the Congress, but allowed 159 Eastern bishops, all alleged supporters of the Monophysite doctrine, to be present. Few records exist from the meeting and what actually happened is a mystery. Nevertheless, subsequent events soon proved that Justinian's agenda of establishing the Monophysite Doctrine had been attained.

Evidence indicates that as a result of the Congress, many of the early Gospels were altered to remove all references to reincarnation. Orthodox versions of the Old and New Testaments written after the Congress reflect these deletions; so in reading these, we are not privy to the teachings of the earlier scriptures. Fortunately, many surviving manuscripts written prior to the sixth century remain intact and therefore provide great insight into the original teachings of Christianity.

In addition to altering the Gospels, arguments over the nature of Christ escalated during the Congress. Five hundred years later, in 1054, the Roman and Greek Catholic Churches excommunicated each other. Differences between these Church philosophies are still evident today.

Many Eastern religions, such as Hinduism and Buddhism, on the other hand, freely embody notions of reincarnation, and as world cultures permeate one another, Westerners are ever more exposed to these ideas on a daily basis. The most recent search for the newly reincarnated Dalai Lama, for example, received worldwide as well as national publicity.

Slowly people are beginning to re-examine the dogma under which traditional Christian churches operate. Translations of the Gospels from original manuscripts are now available. As our exposure to this information grows, more and more people are coming to accept the possibility of the soul's reincarnation.

SPECIAL ANGELS

When I first met a dear friend of mine many years ago, she did not believe in life after death, much less reincarnation. At that time she believed that people had only one chance to live, and then it was over. Since our first meeting, she has given birth to a beautiful little girl whose eyes reflect a very wise, old soul. When her daughter was three years old, she confided to me in hushed, fearful tones that her daughter had been talking about angels and that this worried her.

"Well, what does she say?" I asked.

Looking down at her shoes, she replied with embarrassment, "She insists she used to be an angel before she was born."

I couldn't help but smile. What a beautiful truth this little child was bringing to her mother.

"Did you talk with her about it?" I asked.

"Well, no," she replied. "I ignored it. I don't know what to say, but she still keeps talking about it. She tells me that there are a lot of angels that are born as people, and that we were all angels first. Then last week she told me she wished her name was Julie."

"Oh, that's interesting," I replied. "I wonder who Julie is."

My friend was quiet a moment and then looked up and said, with tear-filled eyes, "That's my sister's name, the one who committed suicide."

I smiled and calmly reassured her, "Your daughter is speaking her truth and she should be honored." I explained that, as parents, we often had to first overcome our own fears to be capable of honoring our children's truth. Thanks to the words of a little angel of her own, my friend now believes in life after death, angels, and even perhaps the possibility of reincarnation.

Many messages of comfort come through our children if we are willing to listen. Christopher once reminded me that he was an angel before he was born again in this lifetime. Puzzled, his brother and sister asked him what he was talking about. He looked at them sternly and in a dismissing tone replied, "I'm talking to Mommy right now."

He then turned back to me and continued, "Mommy, if I die again, then I will be an angel again, and I will come down to visit you in your house. I will always be with you."

Thankfully, I was listening. I had heard those words before, and the comfort they brought me was immeasurable.

Children are unique individuals and require validation of their experiences and memories, even if those memories are seeping in from past lives. To deny these remembrances out of fear or lack of understanding only causes children to internalize the belief that we do not accept all of who they are. And with that belief, their self-esteem plummets.

When children speak a core truth to us and we dismiss it because it sounds implausible when referenced against our everyday existence, we are telling them that their truth, their fears, their loves and their desires are not valid. No adult thrives in an environment in which they are not validated. It is unrealistic to expect our children to thrive in such an environment either.

Open your hearts to the souls of your children. Listen to your little angels as they share their experiences with you. Allow them to be all that they are. Know that you, too, have been in the angelic state and have known truth and experienced unlimited, unconditional love. Do not have fear when they speak of things foreign to you. They have recently been to the place of universal light and love. They have much wisdom and comfort to share with you.

HEALING THE SOUL

Chapter 7

Once we accept the premise that reincarnation is at least possible, then a great deal of healing information can be elicited from our soul's memories. When we think of heredity, we typically think of our genetic ancestors. Of course our bodies inherit our parents' genes, but our spirits transcend this physical boundary. It is our spirit, our *anima*, that infuses us with life. Our spirit is ours alone, not a copy of our parents'. Our souls live on after the body's death and are reborn again and again into new bodies, in new situations, in new lives that enable us to learn and heal our core issues.

In each life, we are free to choose our destiny, how we will behave, what values we will hold and even which thoughts we will entertain. Whether consciously or unconsciously, we are constantly making these choices. We are not genetically destined to become an abuser, a giver, a perfectionist or a co-dependent person. We have choice in life. We are free to choose to actively heal or to continue to remanifest that which needs to be healed. This knowledge can be priceless for the adult children of abusive or dysfunctional parents, as these individuals often fear that they have inherited their parents' tendencies.

Our spirits choose situations to be born into which help heal our core life issues. Core issues are those which are a constant theme in our lives. They are the threads which tie together many of our experiences. A core life issue might be the inability to stand up for yourself, the lack of courage and self-esteem to remove yourself from an abusive situation, the inability to trust others, a pattern of escaping reality through drug or alcohol abuse, or a history of constant betrayal. Often these issues come up for healing in childhood. Unfortunately, children often don't have the tools, guidance or support to effectively deal with them.

Upon reaching adulthood, these unresolved issues continue to present themselves for resolution. We repeatedly set ourselves up, albeit subconsciously, in situations where our soul can learn needed lessons from its experience and manifest resolutions to core issues. The first step in breaking the cycle of repeated, painful situations lies in recognizing the patterns which exist.

Our spirits choose to be reborn in situations that will allow us to learn, understand and heal. The rapist may return as the incest victim to experience abuse from the other side. The abuser may return as the abused child, and the soul who would not claim her own power may return time and time again to learn how.

As a therapist, I have seen hundreds of such clients successfully heal their core issues. I will share several of their stories with you to illustrate the steps necessary to understand your own life issues and facilitate your own healing. The following is an example of how core issues present themselves.

April, a woman in her early twenties, had been physically and sexually abused by her father when she was a child. As an adult, she had recreated the abusive situation by seeking out and marrying a physically and verbally abusive spouse. Why was she born into this situation? What caused her repetitive pattern of abuse and why was she seemingly immobilized in it?

Part of the answer lay in one of April's past lives where she herself had been an abuser. Her soul had chosen to recreate and attract abusive situations in this lifetime in an effort to heal her underlying core issues.

Often people get "stuck" in these repetitive patterns and begin to believe that they will never be happy. This does not have to be the case. We were meant to experience joy and fulfillment. The choice to heal is yours. This book will guide you to the next step in the healing of your soul so you, too, can be happy and whole.

To accomplish that healing, you must first recognize what your core life issues are; then you must be willing to take the actions necessary to heal. Very likely you have already identified one or more recurring patterns in your life that you may be "stuck" in.

Often what keeps us "stuck" in unpleasant experiences is that we have lost the parts of ourselves which embodied characteristics of courage, self-esteem, and will power. Those lost soul pieces, together with the personality characteristics they possessed, would have enabled us to face our core issues and conquer them. So where did that courage, self-esteem and will power go? And how can we get these lost pieces of our souls back?

Let us begin by looking at the ancient concept of *soul loss*. Many cultures, in many eras, have believed that a piece of your soul can split off during times of extreme physical or emotional trauma. Since the soul is with you in all incarnations, a piece could have split off during trauma experienced in this or any lifetime.

To understand how the split-off takes place, it is useful to examine what happens in near-death experiences. People who have reported near-death experiences often relate that they felt as if they were out of body, standing or floating somewhere nearby as they watched their physical body experience the car accident, rape or other traumatic event. In an effort to not suffer such inordinate pain, we momentarily escape our physical bodies in times of extreme duress.

This out of body experience is similar to what happens when we suffer soul loss, except that in soul loss a portion of our soul, a particular density, detaches and remains out of body because it does not want to return. The piece of soul that detaches often does not trust that the situation will get better or perhaps does not believe that the body will survive the trauma. The density of the lost soul part depends on the severity of that trauma. Typically, the more severe the trauma, the greater or denser the amount of soul that leaves.

Civilizations throughout time have recognized the reality of soul loss. Even today, people of many cultures speak of the change in a person's eyes, appearance or personality following a traumatic event, often remarking, "He was just never the same afterwards."

The ancient healing tradition of *soul retrieval* was practiced to heal soul loss. Cultural anthropologists have documented this tradition in many civilizations as far back as 10,000 years ago. Diverse cultures in North America, Australia, Asia and South America all shared similar beliefs about soul retrieval long before any documented cultural exchange between these peoples existed. The similarities extend to depictions, instructions, and descriptions about where you must go to retrieve lost soul pieces, how you get there and the procedure of the retrieval itself.

Put simply, soul loss occurs when a person experiences a physical or emotional trauma so severe that a piece of their soul splits off because it can no longer tolerate the reality of the event. The traditions and cross-cultural techniques of soul retrieval were created so shamans could retrieve these lost pieces and bring them back to be reunited with the rest of the soul.

Years ago when I first heard of this concept, goose bumps spread over me. I knew it would help me heal. In the days that followed, I was directed to an old shaman who practiced these traditional healing methods, and I went to him to have a soul retrieval done.

In a small, quiet room filled with the scent of burning sage, the old man entered his trance as he rhythmically beat his drum. Closing my eyes, I felt the presence of Native Americans all around. Slowly I began to float up out of my body. Feeling perfectly safe, I allowed the sensation to continue, and after passing through a dark fog, I emerged at an Indian village. A fire burned brightly in the center of the village, and a circle of Native Americans welcomed me there. I sat with them until I was told to return.

Upon returning to my body, I found the shaman blowing a soul piece into my heart chakra and then my crown chakra. His ancient eyes smiled as he told me he had brought back a piece from when I was nine years old. He said he found my soul piece huddled on the floor, sure that I had died, and that there had been a man standing there holding our whole family at gun point.

I immediately remembered the scene and was shocked that the old healer had gone there. It was from a petrifying time. During one of my father's rare visits home, he suffered an extremely severe flashback. He had woken up one night, believing that he was in a Korean POW camp, and held the whole family at gunpoint with a twelve-gauge shotgun. In his mind we were the North Koreans. He spoke to us in a mixture of Korean and English, vowed he was going to escape, and threatened to kill any of us that moved.

I was literally frozen with fear. Mom stepped forward, talking to him calmly. Dad reacted by thrusting the loaded gun to her head. That must have been when the soul piece split off. I remember closing my eyes, believing with all my heart and soul that we were going to die.

Miraculously, we all survived. Somehow Mom's unflinching reassurances got Dad back in touch with reality. He broke down on the floor sobbing, in a heap of sweat and tears, terrified by his own loss of control and the danger into which he had put his family.

I looked into the eyes of the old shaman who had brought part of me home again and asked, "What happens now?"

"You must integrate the piece I have brought back to you," the shaman replied. "Honor its presence, acknowledge its needs and for a while indulge its desires. In the past, entire communities would celebrate the return of a lost soul piece; now the old ways have changed and we must do this individually."

The return of my nine-year-old piece, and the integration of its character strengths, catapulted me forward on my own path to empowerment. Later, I learned to do soul retrieval myself and incorporated it into my practice, where it quickly proved effective for those clients whose healing required more than the traditional tools of psychotherapy. Moreover, I soon realized that retrieving lost soul parts could literally mean the difference between life and death.

RETRIEVING THE WILL TO LIVE

*L*ate one night, I received an urgent phone call from one of my clients whose eleven-year-old nephew from Guatemala was in critical condition due to a motorcycle accident. I hurried to the Medical Center to see what I could do.

The boy's father, who had been driving the motorcycle, had been killed, and the little boy's pelvis had been run over by an oncoming bus. Emergency surgery, which included screwing plates into his severely broken pelvis, had been performed in Guatemala City to save his life, but his condition continued to decline. At that point his mother decided to life-flight him to the Houston Medical Center.

The boy, Manuel, had been in Houston for two days and was not responding to treatment. A large subcutaneous sac of fluid had formed just above his sacrum, and the doctors were unable to determine its cause. Theories ranged from spinal fluid leakage, to urine, to fluids resulting as a rejection of the metal pins and plates. The boy was in extreme pain, not eating and, worst of all, not recovering. Manuel's life force continued to slip away and it seemed traditional Western medicine could do no more.

Standing at his bedside, his mother's desperation was obvious. I asked her to have a seat as I quietly moved to the foot of his bed. Manuel, who was in a drug-induced sleep, was not aware of my presence. As I laid my hands on his feet, healing energy began to flow through me, and our energy bodies merged. I was immediately taken to the scene of the accident. Tears streamed down my face as the scene of the bus running over him played itself out before my eyes over and over again. The morphine in his body made my head spin, and I felt nauseated to the point of vomiting. My pelvis was filled with crushing pain as I remained in his energy body.

The intensity of my physical reactions rapidly became unbearable, and I finally prayed to not experience so much on that level. Gratefully, the sensations I was picking up from Manuel soon subsided, and I was able to continue my work.

I stood at the foot of his bed channeling healing energies deep into his body for two hours. When the work was complete, the little boy opened his eyes, slowly lifted his hand, reached behind him, and gingerly felt his pelvis. Manuel smiled up at his mother, and said, "It's gone."

His mother wept with joy and relief. Overwhelmed with gratitude, she hugged and kissed me. The swelling had receded, and the throbbing pain had vanished.

Only a week had passed when I received another desperate phone call. Manuel was dying. The doctors did not know what was wrong. He was refusing to eat, take his medicine, or talk to anyone. Worse, his body was not responding to the liquid diet that was being force-fed through a tube in his nose. I arrived at the hospital late that night to begin my work. I knew it could not wait until morning.

I looked at the gaunt shell of the little boy and nearly wept. He looked as if he had been in a concentration camp. The mere skeleton of a child lay sleeping, curled up on his side, pain etched into his face. He was breathing only shallowly, waiting for death to release him.

His mother's despair filled the air as she explained that he had just been given more pain medicine and it always made him sleepy.

"That's all right," I said. "He doesn't need to be awake for this."

I looked into the eyes of his frightened mother and asked, "Do I have your permission to do whatever needs to be done?"

"Yes, yes," she pleaded. "Do anything. I can't bear to lose my son. I have already lost my husband. But, could my sister and I stay in the room with you?"

"Of course," I replied.

They took a seat on the couch near the window. I took a candle out of my bag, and as I lit it, I said a prayer releasing my work to God. Then, quietly I placed the guest chair next to his bed and sat cross-legged upon its cushion. Placing my hands on him, I immediately entered a deep shamanic trance.

Once again I was taken to the scene of the accident. It was where I had expected to go. A piece of Manuel's soul, resembling a light colored shadow, stood in the road watching the bus run over his body. Time and again, the scene replayed. I went over to the lost soul piece, explained who I was and said that it was time to go home.

"No," he said. "There is no where to go. Manuel has died. Look," he said, pointing to the body lying in the road. "You see, the bus ran over me and my body is dead. No one could live through that."

"But you did, Manuel. You lived and you must come back with me in order to help your body heal." After several minutes of reassuring the young soul piece that his body had indeed survived, he finally agreed to come back with me.

As soon as I took his hand, however, I was led into an abyss, black as coal. There I found two more pieces of Manuel's soul that had been lost within days of each other. They were standing side by side in the dark holding onto a tiny burning match. I knew they were post-accident pieces, but wasn't shown what had caused them to split off. All I sensed was that they were filled with fear.

I quickly whisked them out of the dark. Suddenly I found myself in the tunnel through which souls often pass after death on their way to the Light. I was not surprised that part of Manuel's soul had entered the transition tunnel, but I was surprised at how far through the tunnel it had gone. In previous journeys, I had gone to the tunnel to retrieve soul parts which people had lost when loved ones died, and they wanted to go with them. But usually the lost part was no more than halfway.

This time I walked three-quarters of the way through the tunnel before I finally saw Manuel at the end, standing in the Light. This proved to be the hardest piece to get back. I called to him and asked him to return with me.

"No," he replied. "My father is here and I want to stay with him. I love him."

"I know you love him, Manuel, and he knows it, too. But it's very important that you come with me now so that you can heal and live."

He adamantly refused. Round and round we went. I wanted to walk further toward the Light and take him by the hand, but I could not get any closer. I showed him his three other soul pieces, and he finally, reluctantly, agreed to come. I cried as I watched him give his father a sorrowful goodbye hug and sadly walk slowly back through the tunnel towards me. I understood his grief, but this was the piece that would bring life back to Manuel.

I returned from my meditative state back in the hospital room and eased the re-entry of Manuel's split-off soul pieces into his little body. Though he was still in a drugged sleep, his entire body began to tremble. Alarmed, his mother came over and wanted to know if she should call the doctor.

"No," I replied. "Let me steady his energy body, and he'll be fine."

Within a few minutes, Manuel was calm. He still slept, but now lay relaxed and smiling, breathing deeply and at peace. What a change! I asked his mother to call me in the morning and let me know how he was doing. When I checked my messages the next day, I learned that Manuel was up, eating everything in sight and even arguing with the nurses. I am happy to report that Manuel has since made a marvelous recovery. He is walking well again and delighting everyone with his sense of humor.

Manuel was, at heart, a basically happy child. His great love for his father, however, had prompted his will to die along with his father. For many, however, losing the will to live stems from other circumstances. One of the most profound soul recoveries I've ever done was for a fifteen-year-old named Frank. The force that fueled his will to die was far more frightening.

CONQUERING SUICIDE

Frank was a smug, defiant young man who had serious substance abuse problems and talked constantly of his desire to burn himself so he could experience ultimate pain before he died. By the time he came to see me, he had already used hot coat hangers to burn words such as "loco" into various parts of his body. His father brought him to me as a last resort when the psychiatric hospitals had not helped and the medications prescribed had no effect on his instability.

Frank told me there was no such thing as a loving God. If there was, he said, his parents would not have divorced, and his fingers would not have been ripped off by the saw in woodshop. He felt life just wasn't worth living if there was any un-happiness involved in it at all, even if it was only five minutes a day.

I asked him if he would mind doing a simple energy clear-ing. He agreed, but told me in no uncertain terms that it would not work and that he was not going to change his mind about committing suicide.

"That's fine," I said. "I appreciate you humoring me."

We began by doing an emotional clearing and forgiveness work with regard to his parents that released unprocessed emotions which were clogging his energetic body. Then I channeled energy back into his thymus gland to boost his body's innate will to live. I knew a small part of him still wanted to live or he would not have participated in the session at all. We talked a while and scheduled another appointment for the following day.

Frank was a child who had suffered huge soul loss and was filled with anger. I also sensed intuitively that his desire to kill himself transcended this lifetime and involved past life issues as well. Investigating his past lives would be the key to under-standing Frank's present problems, but doing soul retrieval would be the key to his survival.

As our scheduled appointment approached, I began to feel an unusual sense of apprehension and danger. I kept telling myself I was being ridiculous. What could present itself in Frank's case that I had not seen before? Despite my repeated attempts to dismiss these intuitive warnings with reassuring thoughts, my sense of danger continued to grow.

That afternoon Frank arrived at my office with an attitude of resolute arrogance. "I'm here," he said, "but I'm not going to let you help me because I don't want to get well."

"That's fine," I said agreeably. "I accept how you feel, and I appreciate you coming to see me one more time."

I sat down across from him, smiled and said, "What I want to do today is something a little different. I want to do a form of ancient healing work with you." I briefly explained soul retrieval and asked his permission to do the work.

Frank reluctantly agreed, and I began my preparations. I was guided to do a ceremony filled with ritual so that he would have something tangible to hold on to. I began by performing the ancient cleansing ritual of smudging with the pungent smoke from burning sage. I smudged the room, Frank, my drum, the blanket, and myself. I then lit ceremonial candles, reverently placing them in the four cardinal directions of Native American traditions.

As Frank lay down on the blanket, I stood and encircled us with a fine line of cornmeal, making a Sacred Circle of Life to further protect me on my journey. At last I began to sing my sacred song. I sat down cross-legged next to Frank, touched his arm gently with my knees and began drumming. Releasing my work to God, I immediately slipped into a deep meditative state and found myself in the family room of a house looking at a five-year-old soul piece of Frank's. This piece felt rejected and came back with me readily when I held my arms out to him. I later learned that Frank's mother had breast-fed him until he was five, and I surmised that the sense of rejection this piece felt must have occurred when she stopped.

After this, a most unusual thing occurred. I was told it was important for me to know of one of Frank's past lives so I could understand what was causing him so much torment. Frank, from a previous lifetime, then appeared before me as a man in his early twenties with dark hair, a small frame, and a deranged look in his eyes. He said he wanted to kill himself because he needed to be punished.

"Why do you need to be punished?" I asked.

"Because of all the people I've killed," he replied emphatically.

The crazed look in his eyes turned to pain and a cold wind rushed over me as he began to describe how he had tortured, mutilated and brutally murdered several women.

When he was through, I explained to him that he had not been psychologically well when he did those things and that it was now time to forgive himself. He listened, but found it difficult to fully accept that he was worthy of forgiveness. Hesitantly, he agreed to think about what I had said.

As I surrounded him in white light, clarity came to me as to why Frank had mutilated himself and wanted to commit suicide by fire. The mutilation was his effort to reconnect with his past life, even to the extent of branding the word "loco" on his forearm. The desire to burn himself reflected his desire to purify and cleanse himself while simultaneously eliciting the punishment he felt he deserved.

As I contemplated these insights, I re-entered the traveling stage of my journey, but immediately got stuck in a gray area and was not allowed to go on. I repeatedly restated my intent to go forward to retrieve the soul pieces that would help Frank heal, but I kept hearing, "No."

"Yes," I firmly responded. "I know I am safe to go where I need to go. I am the Light and the Light always wins over the Darkness. I am ready to make this journey."

Each time the reply came back, "No."

Three times I reaffirmed my intentions and then slowly I felt the five-year-old piece I had retrieved being taken from my side by a guide.

"I will watch over him while you are gone," he said solemnly. "Have faith."

Out of the fog, a boat appeared. There was no one in it. It reminded me of an ancient Viking boat. I approached the water and climbed aboard. Slowly the boat began to move across the dark water. I had an uncomfortable, eerie sense that I was leaving everything behind. For the first time in all my many journeys, I felt completely alone. Despite the murky darkness, I could still see; but the eerie blackness was not just lack of light, it was dark energy seeping in and around every atom. Never before, on any journey, had I encountered such a strange blackness.

After some time, the bow of the boat slid up on shore with a lurch. As I stood up to get out, I could see I had landed on a small island. To my horror, I saw numerous dark energy bodies in frenzied pursuit of soul pieces desperately fleeing their attackers. When caught, the dark entities sucked the life force out of the helpless pieces.

Once the Light had been completely sucked out of a soul piece, the piece actually died and would be of no use to retrieve except to torture someone. The horrific zeal with which these dark beings extracted the life force from their victims can only be compared to scenes from the Holocaust where torturers received joy and satisfaction from brutal, inhumane extermination. Shockingly repulsed, I named this place "The Island of Death."

I quickly surveyed the island for Frank's soul piece and found him lying on the ground on the right side of the island. As I started toward him, I realized I no longer had my usual strength. Far more energy than normal was required just to walk over to where he was lying. Frank's piece was very dark, almost dead. I attempted to revive it, but was powerless to do so. I attempted to channel Light into his soul piece, but no Light would come. I tried to lift him so I could take him back to the boat and revive him there, but my arms were too weak.

I was powerless to do the simple things I normally did with ease. Worse yet, the longer I was there, the more I felt my own energy drain away. I was tempted to just lie down and rest, but I knew that would mean certain death.

I quickly prayed for help. No help came. I felt a small twinge of fear in my chest as I realized I was completely, utterly on my own. Black flying energy bodies were hovering over me now, like vultures waiting for their prey to fall. I closed my eyes, and repeated emphatically and without fear, "I am the Light, the Light is in me and the Light always wins!" Immediately I knew what to do. I bent down, focused all my strength on Frank's soul piece and began to push and roll him toward the shore. In my weakened state, he felt like he weighed 400 pounds. The flying energies were so close I could feel the cold they radiated as they whizzed by.

Then, two hard hits penetrated my back. The indescribable pain was consuming and excruciating. I fought to remain focused as the attack continued. I knew I had to reach the shore or I would die. Searing pain raced down my right leg. I dropped to my knees and used the strength remaining in my left side to keep pushing Frank's soul piece toward the shore.

At last, I reached the water. Even in that cold, dark water I felt safer than I did on the island. Frank's soul piece was much lighter in the water, and I was able to float him over to the boat. Knowing I lacked the strength to lift him, I carefully lashed his body to the side of the boat with a piece of rope I found lying inside the open hull. Then, summoning all my remaining energy, I threw my leg over the side of the boat and pulled myself in. As the boat slowly began to slip away from shore, I lifted my head to look back one last time at that dreadful island. I felt drained, as if dark leaches had sucked the life force itself out of me. I was grateful to still be alive.

The boat rocked gently in the soft waves and, after what seemed like hours, we arrived at the other shore. Several guides, who appeared to me as Native Americans, were standing on the beach waiting for me. As light from a warm fire flickered across their faces, I could see their expressions of relief.

"He's almost dead," I said. "Please help me revive him."

Two guides quickly carried Frank's soul piece to shore and began to work on him. As I looked on from the boat, too tired to lift myself out, I was relieved to see Frank's piece being replenished with the life force he so desperately needed. Exhausted, I closed my eyes and rested. A short while later, I heard footsteps approaching. One of my teachers had arrived. He smiled at me with paternal eyes that clearly showed his worry.

"How are you my child?"

"Tired," I said, "but very happy."

As he extended his hands to help me out of the boat, he said, "You did good work, but we were not sure you were ready to go. Why were you so insistent?"

"I really wanted to help this boy. I knew he didn't have enough of his soul with him in this life to hold onto the will to live. I had no idea his lost soul piece was in such a horrific place," I said, nodding in the direction of the island.

Soberly, my teacher looked down into my eyes and said, "The Island of Death is a most dangerous place for a Light worker to be, because you must go in all alone. You have no help when you are there, and you lose more and more power the longer you stay. We have lost many warriors to the dark forces on the island. You must rest now. Come with me."

With an arm around my waist to help me walk, he led me over to the fire. I lay down on a blanket and fell asleep. When I awoke, there were two wolves lying next to me, warming me. My teacher smiled and said, "It is time for you to go now, my child. The boy's pieces are ready to return."

I thanked my friends for taking care of me and for helping me with Frank. Moments later, Frank's soul pieces appeared by my side, and we made our journey home. Back in the room with Frank's temporal body, I blew the soul pieces into him, sealed them in and leaned back to rest. It had been like a strange journey from a Carlos Castaneda book, and I felt as if I'd been trampled by a herd of horses. Every muscle in my body hurt.

"That was weird," Frank said when it was over. "As I was laying here with my eyes closed, I kept seeing Indians."

I smiled and said, "I know, Frank."

I related the events of my journey and told him how to welcome his pieces back. He didn't seem to be much affected, and I prayed that God would allow him to feel what he needed to feel in order to heal. I asked Frank to promise that he would wait two weeks to allow my work to take effect before he acted on his suicide decision. Once again, he reluctantly agreed.

The journey had been physically hard on me. I felt sick and struggled with an excruciating backache. After a few days, the physical symptoms eased, but I was not anxious to ever return to the Island of Death.

A week went by, and on Sunday I had a call from Frank. "I have to talk to you," he said urgently. "I've made some decisions, and I want to share them with you. Do you have time to see me?"

"I always have time to see you, Frank," I replied. "Why don't you come over at three?"

"That's great," he said. "I'll be there."

The buzzer in my office sounded promptly at three o'clock announcing Frank's arrival. As I entered the waiting room, I saw a boy I had never seen before. His eyes had life. He looked profoundly different.

His smiling father stood a few feet behind him. "I'll let you two talk. Just beep me on my pager when you're done."

"Come in," I said to Frank. "Have a seat. What's going on?"

"It all happened on Wednesday," he began excitedly. "I don't know how to explain it, but something just changed. I want to live. I think the average male life expectancy of seventy-four is much too short for all the things I want to do!"

I could not believe what I was hearing. This was a monumental shift. It was much bigger than I had ever expected.

"I've decided I want to be a healer," he continued exuberantly. "I want to help children who are in trouble like I was. I've also decided to go to a special school for a semester so I can get caught up on all my failed classes and graduate with my friends, and my sister found me a job as a busboy! I'm so excited!"

He went on and on for over an hour, then said he was hungry and asked permission to raid the office pantry. We went to the lunchroom, and I sat there in amazement as I watched this vibrant fifteen-year-old devour a huge bag of chips while enthusiastically telling me about his plans for life.

A miracle had truly occurred in this child, and I was honored to have played a part in the facilitation of his healing. I'm pleased to report that Frank is now a healthy college student with no substance abuse problems and a bright future.

PAST LIVES – PRESENT PAIN

*A*fter the Island of Death experience, I asked to be shown a new, safer way to accomplish soul retrievals. I was guided to leave the traditional rituals behind and soon began practicing what I call Enlightened Shamanism. My new healing modality, Enlightened Shamanism involved an entirely different method of "journeying," centered in universal light, love and faith.

The power for healing through Enlightened Shamanism far exceeds that of traditional shamanism. Traditional soul retrieval, for example, typically heals soul loss from this lifetime. With Enlightened Shamanism, however, lost soul pieces can be retrieved from past as well as present lives through a process I call *soul recovery.*

Enlightened Shamanism, in all its aspects, represents a synergy of various healing modalities. Clairvoyant abilities are combined with specific ancient healing techniques, hypnotherapy, past life regression, meditation, and healing on the astral plane.

Additionally, these methods are employed within a framework of quantum physics, which holds that time is not linear. This type of journeying represents an ephemeral, or momentary, retrofusion of time. It is a temporary fusion of the past and the present. By bringing the past into the present, it once again becomes the present, and is therefore malleable and open to change. When open to change, it is open to healing. Applying these principles, in combination with the concept of reincarnation, has created vast healing opportunities.

My method of soul recovery became unlike anything that I had studied or read about before. The journey was accomplished through astral travel. No drums were required, and, thankfully, there were no more demons to fight. As my proficiency increased, I was catapulted into areas I wasn't aware existed. I discovered that soul recovery could span lifetimes. More importantly, for many people past life soul recovery is crucial in certain instances for healing to occur.

Our soul's memories of past life experiences do not necessarily cease when we are reborn. These memories are often re-experienced in dreams which bridge the gap between current reality and the subconscious. In doing so they provide clues for our healing. One client, June, had had a recurring dream for over twenty years in which a man with a knife was chasing her. Despite her best efforts, she could never escape his attack. Ultimately, each time, he would catch her and kill her. Her dreams were so vivid she could feel the knife blade penetrating her lungs and abdomen as he repeatedly plunged the dagger into her body.

Dreams such as these are often connected with past life soul loss. Perhaps you, too, can remember a dream you had that was so real, so lifelike that you had a hard time shaking it after waking up, because it seemed as if it had actually happened.

One of my recurring dreams began when I was five and continued regularly for years. In this morbid dream, I would abruptly beam into a WWII battle scene. Filled with shock and horror, I watched the soldiers under my command being cut down in an ambush. Finally, after being struck by a bullet myself, I collapsed to the ground. As the final breath of air left my lungs, I remember being overwhelmed with a sense of guilt and responsibility for having led these men to their deaths.

I always awoke from these incredibly realistic dreams gasping for air to refill my lungs, surprised that I had not actually died. Then, for hours I would lay awake, drenched in cold sweat, as the faces of my dead men continued to reappear before my eyes.

Where could those images have come from? At that point in my life, I had never been permitted to see a World War II movie. Because of the Vietnam War, my mother would not turn on the radio or television in an effort to shield me from the harsh realities of war. So it is safe to say these dreams were not influenced by outside exposure. These dreams turned out to be very special, but it took almost twenty years from their first occurrence for me to realize that they held the key to a physical symptom I manifested as an adult.

In my mid-twenties, I began experiencing a sharp, continuous pain in my forehead, and after a few months, I noticed a bone growth in that region. Fearing bone cancer, the doctors took X-rays, ran an M.R.I., and finally operated, only to find a benign area of growth they could not explain. Yet, even two years after the growth's removal, the pain persisted.

Since I was seeing patients with inexplicable chronic pain in my practice, I decided to explore my own area of pain on a deeper level. I sensed that the pain transcended what I was experiencing in this lifetime, therefore, I decided to delve into my subconscious for clues as to what was causing it.

Caught in the Crossfire

As I entered my meditative state, I felt as if I were drifting back in time. Abruptly, I came out of what appeared to be a tunnel into the World War II battle scene I had dreamt of as a child. This time, however, it was the morning before the battle, and the sun had not yet risen. The light was dim and gray, and a misty fog was rolling in. As an observer, I saw myself in that lifetime as the platoon leader who had been given the order to take the next hill. Suddenly, painfully, I was slammed into the body I had been watching. It seemed that once again I was to re-experience this tragedy.

The air was damp and cold. I was told by my commanding officer that we would encounter no resistance, but my intuition told me otherwise. Everything in my body and spirit told me to disobey the order, but I was a soldier. I had no choice.

I called my men over and gave the order to move forward. Slowly, in the gray dawn, we moved out.

I'll never forget the sick feeling in my stomach when I saw the flashes of light burst forth from the bushes. Hearing the rapid-fire crack of gun shots, I witnessed my men falling all around me. There was no place to run, no way to escape. Once again I saw the men I had ordered into battle look up at me for help as the life slipped out of them. Suddenly, I felt a bullet slam into my forehead, and my body sank to the ground. I was sick with guilt for having led these men to their deaths because I had not had the courage to follow my intuition.

After the soldier died, I once again slipped out of his body. This time from a position of Enlightened Shamanism, I was able to remain at the site and survey the bloody battlefield. To my surprise, I saw a soul piece that had split off from the soldier before he had died. Finally, I knew why I was here. I had come back to this moment in time to retrieve this piece.

The whitish colored energy body, which looked just like the soldier, walked slowly over to me. Still apparently in shock, he told me his name was John. I explained to him that I had come from the future and that I needed him in my present lifetime in order to be whole. He said he could not leave until he had buried his men. I told him I would stay and help him. Using a small shovel, like those used to dig foxholes, we painstakingly dug the graves, set up markers and prayed over each fallen soldier. It was an incredibly sad, yet emotionally cathartic experience. My lost soul piece was finally getting the closure it needed to heal.

John's body was the last to bury, and as I looked at it, I was amazed to see that the bullet had entered the forehead exactly where I was having pain in my present life. I was guided to remove the bullet before we buried the body. Using a narrow knife, John's lost soul piece looked on, as I dug deeply into the body's cranium and carefully extracted the slug. Holding the bloody slug in my hand, I realized its removal would help heal my present existence, for in removing the bullet, I symbolically removed the guilt John incurred as a result of the experience. Once all the graves were finished, we stood together, silently surveying the scene. At last, John said he was ready to return with me. He took my hand, and we came home.

The integration of John took almost a month. An internal dialogue with him became a familiar part of my day, and I was grateful to have him back. He brought me inner strength, helped balance the male and female aspects of my energy and gave me added courage to follow my intuition. He made it very clear, that because he had been a soldier in his lifetime and was bound to follow orders, he had not had the choice to follow his intuition. It cost him his life as well as the lives of his men. I assured him that in this present lifetime, I had the right to choose whether or not to follow my inner knowing.

Having retrieved the part of my soul that was John, gave me additional faith to trust my intuition and proactively exercise choice in life. I am also happy to say that my World War II nightmares have ceased, as well as the pain in my forehead.

Wilderness Attack

Janet was a client who came to me with a problem similar to my own. For years she had suffered from sharp searing pain just below her left shoulder blade. Janet had exhausted every avenue that Western medicine offered in hopes of finding the cause of the pain. But, in the absence of any conclusive indication of abnormality in the region, her doctors could find no cause and were only able to offer symptomatic treatment through physical therapy, pain pills and muscle relaxants. By the time she came to see me, her left arm was partially immobilized due to the severity of the pain. She was quite receptive to my suggestion that we look into her past life experiences since there was no apparent cause for the pain she presently suffered.

Janet opted to "journey" with me so she could see and experience what I saw. Soon after we began, we arrived at a wooded scene in what appeared to be North America in the early 1700's. Janet recognized herself as a buckskin clad male settler who was hurriedly walking alone through the forest. He had a beard, long dirty hair and appeared to be in his early thirties. As we followed him, we were startled when Native Americans suddenly burst out from behind the trees and attacked him. After a short futile battle, he was struck in the back with a hatchet, just below the left shoulder blade.

We walked up to the body, and I instructed Janet to remove the hatchet, place her hand over the deep, bloody wound and channel Light to heal it. I then asked her to turn to the Native Americans and forgive them for having taken his life. I told her she needed to understand that this was a time of war and that the Native Americans were fighting for land that was rightfully theirs. This understanding made it easier for her to forgive.

After the forgiveness work was done, a frightened soul piece emerged from behind a tree. Seeing that all was safe, he cautiously walked over to Janet and gave her a warm embrace. She held him tightly as we journeyed home.

After our session, Janet was flooded with memories from the time period. The man she had been then was called David and had lived during the years before America's independence. She also knew that David had left behind a wife and children, and she was able to give a detailed description of their wooden house.

Janet's healing work on David's wound had apparently been immediately effective, because following the session, her shoulder pain was completely gone. I asked her to call and check in with me in a few days to see how she was doing. Three weeks later, Janet reported that her shoulder remained pain free, but even more important than that was her incredible joy to be alive! It has been several years now since Janet and I did this work, and she still reports being free of shoulder pain. She also believes that reconnecting with the aspect of her soul that was David changed her life. Now that she has reintegrated his energy, she has an appreciation of life and for being alive that she never had before.

FEARS AND PHOBIAS

O f all human emotions, fear has the greatest potential to limit, if not paralyze, our lives. As in the case of Christopher's fear of alligators, past life events may well explain the existence of strong, illogical fears for which there are no apparent causes in this life. Because the intensity of the emotions we associate with mortal danger are so strong, it is relatively easy for the fears we have associated with past life danger, trauma and dying experiences to bleed through into our present consciousness.

Aquaphobia

Darlene, a woman in her late fifties, came to see me to conquer her fear of water. She had been petrified of it for as long as she could remember. As a child, she never took baths or swam, and as an adult she could not sit in a Jacuzzi. Darlene had just purchased a beautiful new home with a whirlpool bathtub and decided now was the time to conquer her fear.

Over the years, she had been to various therapists who had attempted to overcome her aquaphobia through the process of progressive desensitization. For example, progressive desensitization for a snake phobia may include first talking about snakes, then looking at snake pictures, reading books about snakes, viewing live snakes and ultimately touching and holding snakes. While this method can be effective in dealing with a variety of phobias, it did not, unfortunately, help Darlene. Try as she would, she was still unable to control her fear enough to immerse herself in water.

I talked at length with her, and learned that there were no drowning incidents or frightening events concerning water in her present life. Consequently, I suspected that past life issues were involved, and we proceeded to do a soul recovery. What I found was certainly different than what I had expected. When I arrived upon the scene, I first noticed concentric circles on some kind of surface. As my eyes came into focus, I realized that I was looking down at water. It was lightly raining, but the pool of water was still quite clear. As I looked in wonder at the ripples of concentric circles initiated by each tiny raindrop, I began to gaze more deeply into the water. With an eerie sense of foreboding, I visually searched the bottom of the clear pond. And then I saw it – the bluish-white body of a girl lying motionless on the bottom.

Immediately I checked to see if the body was Darlene's in a previous life, but it was not. Not seeing anyone else around, I checked again. But, no, the body was definitely someone else's. "Look around the shore," I heard. And there, standing on a grassy bank, was a person looking at the body and sobbing uncontrollably. That was Darlene! I had expected her to be the drowning victim, but instead she had suffered the tragic loss of a loved one.

I went over to Darlene's soul piece and explained that the person she missed so dearly had gone on to the Light, and that she may very well know that person in this lifetime. Darlene's past incarnation found such joy in that possibility that she eagerly agreed to come with me. The reunion with today's Darlene was exuberant. The woman who had come to me in despair became as excited as a five-year-old child.

When I saw her next, Darlene had enthusiastically reintegrated the character strengths of her lost soul piece and had completely overcome her phobia. She proudly told me that she had been swimming in a river in New Mexico. She said that not only had she gone swimming, but had also totally immersed herself in the river and let the water flow over her. Darlene apparently went on to have quite a "return to nature" experience. She spent two days outside by the river and laughingly revealed that she even felt compelled to relieve herself in the water!

Darlene's intense fascination with water has now subsided, and she happily uses her whirlpool bathtub and enjoys going swimming with her young granddaughter.

Sometimes, as in the case of Madelaine, whose story I will share with you next, the residual fears we hold as a result of past life experiences are also intertwined with the repetitive patterns we manifest. When we become "stuck" recreating the painful dramas associated with our core issues, soul recovery can be a vital element in healing. Moreover, those lost parts often embody the character strengths we need to face our issues and end our "stuck" patterns.

Russian Blood

Madelaine came to see me soon after divorcing a man who had had numerous affairs during their marriage. Because he had not practiced safe sex in his infidelities, she felt he had been deliberately trying to kill her. Her anger at his betrayals persisted even after the divorce, coupled with an ever-growing aversion to wearing anything that touched her neck. During our second session, Madelaine decided she wanted to try soul recovery to help her regain her ability to trust men and move on with her life.

As I began my journey, I was amazed to find myself recklessly racing down a dark tunnel filled with boulders and jagged rocks. When I emerged from the tunnel, I passed through a dark zone and entered some sort of government compound. There was a wall around the perimeter and what appeared to be a headquarters building in the center. Dust from the ground covered my shoes as I walked closer to the two soldiers that were standing nearby. Suddenly, one soldier pulled a large knife out of a sheath, which was attached to his belt, lunged forward and slashed a gaping cut across the other's throat. Blood gushed out, and as the bleeding body fell to the ground, I watched as a part of its soul split off and stood staring in total disbelief at the betrayal.

The air was cold and it was dark. The murderer stood spattered in blood surveying his victim with great satisfaction. I walked over to the traumatized spirit standing beside its fallen body and recognized it as Madelaine's soul piece.

I told him, "I must take you back. Madelaine needs you."

"I can't believe he killed me! He's my best friend," the stunned spirit cried.

"I know," I said, "but we really must go now. Madelaine is not complete without you. She needs your strength and courage. She needs your ability to trust."

"But he betrayed my trust."

"I know he did, but you knew how to trust, and that's what Madelaine needs. Please come with me now."

Reluctantly, he placed his large hand in mine, and we went home. As I blew his spirit back into Madelaine's heart chakra she began to quiver. She sat up, and before I could even tell her what had happened and who I had found, she exclaimed, "He's so big, it feels like he's stretching my skin! Oh no, my body's not big enough for him!"

After the initial adjustment, she calmed down and closed her eyes as she repeated to me what he was communicating to her. Weeping softly, she said his name was Borris, and that his best friend had killed him in a last ditch struggle for power at the end of the Bolshevik Revolution. As he continued to tell her the details of his life, Madelaine became more and more certain that her husband in this lifetime was the reincarnation of the friend who had slit her throat during the Revolution.

All at once, everything in her present life made sense. It explained why her ex-husband's present day betrayals through infidelities and unsafe sexual practices triggered the fear that this soul would once again take her life. Furthermore, it explained her phobia of things touching her neck. Subconsciously, she was trying to reconnect with this piece in an effort to heal her soul loss.

Suddenly, in the middle of the story she was relating, she opened her eyes and said in a powerful, husky voice, "Do you have a beer?"

"Let's go see," I said.

I, not being a drinker, quickly got up, and led Madelaine down the hall to the kitchen. Looking in the refrigerator, I hoped one might have been left behind from an office party. "Why yes," I replied, relieved to find a lone Heineken.

I'd never known Madelaine to drink beer. She followed me into the lunchroom, walking with a distinct masculine gait. Standing there, she began to look around with amazement. She appeared mesmerized by the appliances and surroundings.

Shaking her head slightly, she finally said, "I feel so disoriented."

"That's normal after soul recovery," I began.

But just as I was about to tell her other common reactions, she suddenly cried, "Bread! Is that bread?"

"Yes," I replied. "Would you like some?"

"Bread! I can't believe it. I am so hungry!"

"Please, help yourself."

I watched as she tore into a slice of whole wheat bread as if she hadn't eaten in days. Then, just as I thought the bizarre behavior was over, she saw a jar of honey on the counter.

"Honey! Is that honey? It's so rare. Can I please have some?" she cried.

"By all means," I replied calmly, wondering what would come next. "Have as much as you like. It's not rare anymore." She quickly poured an enormous amount of honey on her bread, devoured it, and then noisily licked her dripping fingers clean. I could have never imagined this dainty yoga instructor behaving in such a manner! After swigging down the last of her beer, she said she had to go.

A few days later she called to report that her journal writing had become most unusual since her soul retrieval, and that Borris wrote in very poor English and spoke with a Russian accent. She also told me that she felt compelled to wear pants with vests and jackets and enjoyed adorning herself with pins or things resembling medals.

As Borris's character and strengths became more integrated into Madelaine's personality, many things in her life improved. By having the courage to do this work, Madelaine was able to recognize that her fears stemmed from the pattern of repeated betrayal. In doing so, she freed herself from having to remanifest a similar situation again in order to heal this core issue. The pattern could now be broken.

Since her soul recovery, Madelaine is also able to deal with her ex-husband much more effectively. No longer does she shake uncontrollably when she sees him or remain angry for days at a time. She is no longer his victim. She has chosen to live and heal. As an unexpected fringe benefit, Borris also seemed to help Madelaine by giving her the courage and inner strength to lovingly and effectively manage her children.

RELEASING THE GUILT

*I*t is not uncommon in soul recovery to retrieve pieces from lifetimes in which we caused harm to others. In these cases, releasing the guilt or toxic shame is key to moving forward. For some people, it is easier to forgive others than it is to forgive themselves, but forgiveness is crucial. To heal, we must understand ourselves, forgive ourselves and love ourselves unconditionally as God loves us.

Cardinal Sin

Marc came to me with a multitude of relationship issues. Although he had no difficulty getting dates, once in a relationship, the problems began. Marc was capable of intense emotional intimacy, yet had little or no interest in sex. He preferred just being close "friends" with the women he was "dating." He further confided that even sleeping naked with his "girlfriends" had not aroused him, yet he insisted he was heterosexual.

Marc claimed he could go months at a time without ever feeling the desire to initiate sex, and if a woman initiated a sexual advance, it made him feel vulnerable, causing him to immediately shut down and withdraw from the situation. He believed this sense of vulnerability stemmed from an incident where he was "seduced" into having sex by a female friend who subsequently became pregnant and gave birth to his son. Marc and this friend never married, and when she married someone else, he gave up his son for adoption to her new husband.

After several sessions, it became apparent that Marc's habit of remaining sexually distant from women was a lifelong pattern. In his mid-twenties, he had been involved in a five-year relationship with a woman whom he thought he wanted to marry. All during the relationship, which was only infrequently sexual, she continued to see her old boyfriend whenever he came into town. Ultimately, she married the old boyfriend and left Marc feeling rejected and betrayed. I helped him understand that although he may have been emotionally intimate, he was not fully present in the relationship because he had not been physically intimate. Even if she had loved him deeply, after a period of time she was likely to look somewhere else to have her needs met.

Marc had repeated this pattern numerous times. After doing emotional clearings on his present life issues, I suggested we examine his past lives to see if the cause of his present sexual disinterest lay there. He agreed, and we set up a session.

Marc opted to join me as we embarked on our journey back in time. Stepping out of a dense fog, a line of row houses appeared before us. It was England in the late 1800's. Walking across the slippery, cobblestone street, we were directed to a particular house with drawn curtains. As we opened the door, we entered a tiny room lit by a single candle standing on a roughhewn wooden table. Slowly, two shadowy figures became apparent on the left side of the table.

I asked Marc if he could see them.

"Yes," he replied.

"Tell me about them," I said.

"Well, there is a boy about fourteen years old and an adult male."

"Right," I said. "Now, which one are you?"

"I'm the adult male."

"Yes," I replied, as goose bumps covered my body. Marc was fully engaged in the journey and was able to see well. The test, however, was about to come. Could he witness himself in his past life transgression and forgive himself for what he had done?

"Let's go on, Marc. Now, I want you to walk over to these two people and look closely. How are they positioned?"

Marc moved closer to the two figures. "The boy is standing bent over with his hands on the back of the chair and the man is behind him," he said emotionlessly.

"And, can you tell me what they are doing?" I asked.

"Yes, I can," he replied sadly. "The older man is penetrating the boy."

"How does that make you feel," I asked.

"Well, it's wrong. He shouldn't be doing that," Marc responded.

I gently urged him on. "Yes, I know. Marc, what position in society did you have in that lifetime? Were you a teacher?"

"I was a priest. A priest who betrayed his cloth and molested young boys." Marc lowered his head and looked at the ground.

"Can you forgive him, Marc? Can you surround him in universal love and light?"

Marc was silent for a moment. "I can try," he finally said.

The forgiveness of Marc's past life soul piece took quite some time. When he was finished, we closed our session. What we had discovered explained a great deal. Marc had truly re-manifested many facets of his previous life in his present lifetime. He was not a priest this time, but rather a teacher and counselor for adolescent boys. Because he subconsciously did not trust himself to control his sexual urges when he was surrounded by boys, he had shut down his sex drive entirely.

By reconnecting with his past life, Marc was able to heal, release his guilt, face his fears, and admit to himself that he did indeed find males attractive. After embracing his true sex drive, he went on to become fully present in relationships. When he incorporated and integrated the understanding that this healing brought him, Marc was able to bring not only great emotional intimacy to his relationships, but physical intimacy as well.

The Holocaust

Caroline, a rather aggressive young woman from the East Coast, came to me saying that she wanted to have her femininity healed. She told me she was having problems relaxing with her husband during lovemaking and did not feel that she actually deserved his love. Caroline had been sexually abused by her stepfather as a child and claimed to have had several hundred lovers in a variety of circumstances before she was married.

I suspected Caroline had suffered soul loss due to her stepfather's abuse, as well as her own sexual promiscuity. We began our work from this premise. My journey proceeded as anticipated, and I recovered a soul piece of significant density from this lifetime's childhood. I was then unexpectedly thrown into a fog-like mass and taken back in time. Emerging into a scene that was cold, dark and gray, I brought my eyes into focus and saw several structures that resembled military barracks encircled by a tall barbed wire fence. The nauseating stench of death filled the air. A cold chill went up my spine. Where was I?

As I continued to get my bearings, I noticed Caroline's soul piece, who appeared as a man in that lifetime, wearing a Nazi officer's uniform. As I moved closer I saw that he was standing motionless, staring at a huge pile of barely clad, starved corpses. Shock, disgust and guilt lined his face. I went over to talk with him and asked him to come back with me, but he said no, he could never forgive himself for having become involved in the slaughter and for having ordered those deaths.

He was very angry with himself. I continued to talk with him, calmly explaining that it was time to forgive himself, that his soul needed to heal, and that Caroline was a kind person who would understand why he had taken the actions he had. At last, and with great reluctance, he finally agreed to come, placing his cold, clammy hand in mine.

The reaction I observed when this soul piece reconnected with Caroline's body was like none I had ever seen before. She reacted to the retrieved piece before I could tell her what had transpired.

"No! I don't want you! Get out!" she screamed.

I tried to calm her. She was clutching her chest and writing on the floor. Then, without warning, she began to sob hysterically. "My little girl is scared. She's so scared of him!"

She was referring to the little girl piece I had brought back from the abuse in this lifetime. I laid my right hand on her heart chakra to stabilize the area and began to tell her of the pieces that had returned to her. I told her of the German soldier's shame and how she needed to show him love and forgiveness.

"I can't," she growled fiercely. "I don't want him!"

"But he is a part of you, and he will help you heal," I explained keeping my hand on her heart chakra. Anguish covered her face as she tried to accept her newly retrieved pieces. Finally, through gritted teeth she said, "Fine, he can stay, but he has to take off his shoes."

Then, she began talking to her soldier and her little girl. I left the room so she could have time to process alone, and when she emerged, she told me that her German's name was Heinrich, and that he had committed many atrocities. She said that she needed to go home to rest, and that she would communicate with her retrieved pieces through journal writing and meditation.

A few days later, Caroline called to tell me that she believed she had manifested abusive situations in this lifetime in order to experience abuse from a victim's point of view. She felt her soul chose this path in an effort to relieve the pain and guilt she subconsciously carried from Heinrich's actions. She also believed that her self-abuse through sexual promiscuity stemmed from a desire to further connect with Heinrich's guilt by compiling enormous amounts of guilt for her actions in this lifetime. She now understood why when she was visiting

Berlin two years earlier she had been obsessed with buying every old uniform and medal she could find.

To complete her healing process, we did forgiveness work not only on her newly retrieved Heinrich piece, but also on her step-father, and, of course, herself for self-abuse. Today this client has a fabulous love life with her husband, has balanced her male and female energetic aspects and is extraordinarily comfortable in her femininity. Even her wardrobe is reflective of the change. The tall, shiny, black leather boots and long, black leather coats have been replaced with feminine shoes and soft, subtle fabrics which allow her true inner beauty to shine through.

For Caroline and Marc, soul recovery was a critical factor in their healing. They could have spent years in conventional psychotherapy talking endlessly about their feelings, and still never have recovered the strength of character and perspective to understand, forgive and release the guilt which was limiting their present lives.

A BETTER WAY

*M*y clients enthusiastically embraced the powerful results of Enlightened Shamanism, and my practice grew exponentially. Before long the unending flood of individuals seeking
my help was overwhelming. I once again sought a new way – a
more effective way – to heal. I wanted to find a method that
anyone could implement themselves to achieve total healing.

Moreover, the need for a more powerful healing modality
was evidenced by several of my new clients. Beth, a thirty-five
year old heroin addict with three children, desperately needed
help. She was so disconnected, nothing seemed able to reach
her. After a difficult two-week detoxification period, she was

again seeking out the drug. Another client, a twelve-year-old boy, who had just lost two family members in an automobile accident, was unable to function. I was ready and anxious for a better way, a faster more effective way to help my clients.

Two months before I received the Gifts, which you will soon be introduced to, my intuition told me that December 6th was to be a significant day. Try as I might, though, I could not figure out why.

Then late one night the phone call came. I picked up the receiver and heard a husky voice say, "Did I wake you?"

"No," I replied, struggling to recognize the deep male resonance.

"Great! Let's get together."

"Who could it be?" I asked myself.

Through the silence the voice boomed, "It's David. I'm in town and I thought we could get together for dinner or something. I haven't seen you in such a long time."

David was an old friend I'd shared many extraordinary meditations with over the years. Suddenly I was struck with the realization that I had to meditate with David again, not for his benefit, but for mine. "Why?" I wondered. "Why couldn't I get what I needed from meditation without him?" I received no answer, just a firm knowing that I had to meet with him.

The first day we were able to get together was December 6th. We went out for a nice dinner and I shared with him my need to join him in a meditation.

"Any idea why?" he asked.

"No," I replied. "I just know it's something I have to do."

By the time we arrived at home it was late and I was anxious to know what this was all about. We cleared a place on the floor, as an unusual magnetic pull seemed to dictate the very specific body positioning required for this meditation. David was guided to lie down and I sat cross-legged next to him, one knee gently resting against his right thigh and the other touching his arm.

Immediately after closing my eyes to begin my journey, our vibrational levels began to rise with enormous jolts. As David later put it, "Boy, that was a rough take-off!"

And indeed, it was. The adventure that followed was like nothing I had ever experienced, or heard of, before. Feeling as if David and I had been thrown into a blender, our energies were swirling out of control, faster and faster, with ever increasing vibrational frequency. Total release of the journey was the only way to continue. Colors flashed before my eyes as our chakras' energies joined with force. Moments later, at the apex of confusion, with our energetic frequencies soaring higher than I had ever felt before, a phenomenal experience occurred. Our energy bodies fused. We were one.

It was from this incredible point of connection that I was able to travel further out than I ever imagined possible. I was taken to the beginning of time, to the dawning of our universe.

As I arrived at my destination point, I was awestruck by what surrounded me. I watched an incredibly beautiful spiral nebula slowly spinning in space. Stars were streaming, matter was forming, and an array of lustrous colors was pouring forth with a magnificence an artist could only dream of. I was seeing a time before the creation of Earth. Our universe was forming, and the profound power of Creation that surrounded me permeated my entire being. Inner peace, love and knowing filled my soul.

The written word is sorely inadequate to describe the power and ultimate beauty which lay before me. I was so far removed from anything I had ever experienced before. The only thing that made me know I could find my way back home was what appeared to be a single, thin, golden thread binding me to my friend whom I had left behind somewhere as I was catapulted into space.

As I stood watching the spiraling nebula, two guides suddenly appeared. To my surprise, one of them slowly pulled a heavy stone tablet out from behind me. The large, gray tablet stood approximately six feet tall and appeared to be about a foot and a half thick. The other guide formed my right hand into a most unusual *mudra*,[1] which elevated my vibrational level even further, so I could rapidly absorb all the information presented.

Encrypted in the stone were writings in the form of symbols, some of which looked familiar. I knew I had seen this template before. The guide giving the instruction proceeded to explain that the template and its writings originated at the beginning of time. He further explained that the images on the template were a gift from our Creator; a means through which man could reconnect if he ever chose to fully heal. The images and the energetic responses they elicit are our link back home, humanity's golden thread.

The guides further explained that each image acts as a key, activating a counterpart or corresponding encoding within us that unlocks or releases specific healing energies. Image by image, the guides demonstrated how the process worked, and as each image was activated, a golden light radiantly streamed forth. They explained in great detail how this energy was different than any healing energy man had implemented before; that it was a universal energy with healing potential so profound it could bring man back to a state of co-creatorship with the Universe. Man would no longer have to operate from the

---

[1] Hand position.

outside. He would no longer have to ask the Universe to manifest for him. Man, in his healed state, could once again fully participate in the creation process, thereby reconnecting with love, joy and oneness.

As I gazed upon the immense, roughhewn stone, I was told to read from right to left, in ancient form, as the images continued to energize before my eyes. With a sense of urgency, I rapidly tried to absorb all that was before me. The amount of information presented was staggering. I longed to write it down, but the guides assured me I would remember. Then just as suddenly as I had arrived, I was released to return home.

Upon re-entry into my body, I opened my eyes and looked at my friend. Within seconds he, too, returned from his meditative state, and to my surprise, the first words out of his mouth were, "What is soul encoding?"

We talked about our experience for hours before David returned to his hotel. He had not journeyed out as far as I had, and he had not seen the template. However, because we were energetically fused, he had experienced the knowing I had perceived. Recall of the individual images eluded me at that moment, but I trusted they would come to me in due time.

I expressed my deepest gratitude for his presence, for without him as my anchor, I doubt I could have journeyed out that far.

David left town the next day, but weeks passed before our energetic fusion finally disconnected. Until that time we thought each other's thoughts and easily knew what the other was doing, despite the thousands of miles that lay between us.

Soon after his departure, the images I had seen on the template began reappearing to me in meditation. They visually materialized one by one, illuminated in golden light, as I slipped in and out of a meditative state to record what I was being shown. The images, or keys, were then grouped into levels by their function and I was told what healing responses each level elicited.

Three weeks later my instruction was complete, and I was told to entitle the collection of images, Template of Soul I.

I had been shown a new way, a better way. I had been given Gifts that enable each of us to heal ourselves. No longer must we rely solely upon shamans, counselors, therapists or other healing practitioners.

These Gifts allow healing to occur at a phenomenal speed, unattainable until now. I invite you to experience the Gifts and unlock the healing energies within you.

THE GIFTS IN ACTION

---

*A*s the Gifts were revealed to me, my transition from Enlightened Shamanism to what I now call Synergistic Soul Concepts was a rapid one. New insights flooded in and the work progressed with great speed as a leap in the evolution of healing occurred. I applied my new methodologies with phenomenal success. Exponential healing became a reality.

Previous types of images or symbols, such as those utilized by the Maya and Egyptians, conveyed messages or ideas. The Gifts are uniquely different and perform a significantly greater function than mere informational communication. These images actually elicit energetic responses within your body, which set in motion healing processes at the psychological, physio-logical and soul levels.

Healing through the Gifts is unlike chakra-based healing methods such as acupuncture, hands-on techniques, and many modern "new age" alternative therapies. They represent a new way, a new form of healing based on transcendental universal energy which far surpasses the healing capabilities of individual chakra-based energies.

To illustrate the healing power of these Gifts and the re-markable responses typically experienced by those using them to heal, we will follow one client's remarkable journey.

***

Bill, in his early thirties, suffered from a severe case of genital herpes. Breakouts occurred as often as every two weeks. Doctors prescribed the best drugs medicine had to of-fer, and told him there was no cure. He tried various medica-tions to suppress the breakouts, but they were either ineffec-tive or caused serious side effects. Nor were naturopathic supplements or special diets helpful. With no other alternatives in sight, he came to see me.

Bill's background was complex. Abandoned by his mother at one, he never saw her again despite various attempts to con-tact her. His father raised him until he was eight, at which time his father remarried and sent him away to boarding school. Bill suffered from bed wetting until age thirteen. At nineteen he had a homosexual experience where he received felatio. Severe guilt and fear of his own possible homosexuality drove him to marry shortly thereafter.

Throughout his marriage, his fear of bedwetting contin-ued. After eight years of marriage, he contracted herpes. He claimed to have been faithful in his marriage and did not know where he would have contracted the disease. There was, of course, the possibility that his wife had had extramarital involvement, contracted the virus, and transmitted it to him. However, she suffered no symptoms and refused to be tested. He described his home life as incredibly unhappy. After ten years of marriage, he had sought counseling with his wife, which was unsuccessful.

Soon after the attempt at counseling failed, Bill's behavior became self-destructive. Work-related accidents; bicycle, motorcycle and car accidents; as well as drug abuse became normal occurrences in his life. His unconscious death wish was evident as I listened to the story of the last few years of his life, but he still couldn't "see" what he needed to heal. Finally, as his marriage disintegrated, he went so far as to try to find love in the arms of prostitutes. His drinking and drug abuse escalated and took a physical toll. According to his friends, he had aged ten years almost overnight. He was completely out of touch and totally disconnected. He could not understand that to find the love he so desperately desired he had to recognize and fully accept that he was worthy of love.

A traditional psychotherapeutic approach to healing Bill's emotional wounds would have taken years. All the while, he would still have been suffering from herpes, the painful physical manifestation of his deeper issues. If he were to regain his will to live, he would have to address his core issues. Intellectually understanding the cause is one thing, but creating healing at a cellular and spiritual level is quite another. Only through this type of healing can permanent changes in behavior patterns, as well as healing of physical tissue, occur.

Since Bill was an out-of-town client who could not come in regularly, I chose to use the Gifts that I had recently received.

But first, Bill needed a basic understanding of a few underlying concepts and knowledge of how to utilize the Gifts themselves. In this way, he would be empowered to effectively elicit his own healing.

Over the next four months, Bill had a miraculous healing experience. His herpes disappeared, along with the shame associated with his teenage experiences and his worries of again wetting the bed as an adult. Also gone were his fears of latent homosexuality. [Bill experienced a "rebirth," a total reconnection with himself and the Universe. Dramatic changes took place in his life as old core issues were resolved. The self-abuse was over. Bill learned to love himself.] The last time I saw Bill, more than a year after his rebirth, he was still totally clear of the virus. How did this miracle occur? I will share Bill's story with you each step of the way.

⁙

The first session in my office was a lengthy one. I set a cup of steaming green tea on the table in front of Bill and leaned back into my leather chair. Cradling my warm teacup between my hands, I cleared my mind and waited for a knowing of where to begin. Within seconds, the answer came. I took a deep breath, looked across the coffee table at my eager client and began. "Bill, the first concept you need to understand about healing on a soul level is how our souls have evolved."

Bill leaned forward, and I went on to explain, "In the beginning, we were one with the Universe or God. Our separation from God and universal love is addressed in all major religious philosophies."

"Oh yes, I understand," Bill nodded. "In the Bible, for example, our separation from God is described metaphorically in the story of Adam and Eve in the Garden of Eden."

"That's right. And do you know how the separation is depicted in Eastern religious philosophy?"

"Well, if I remember my World Religions class from college, Eastern religions also provide metaphors to describe our choice to separate, but I think they focus primarily on our quest to reunite with God."

"You have a good memory," I said. "Hinduism, for example, maintains that by healing karmic lessons, souls can come full circle and achieve *moksha* or spiritual perfection, thus reuniting with God."

"Right, that's where reincarnation comes in. Each time we come back into a new life we have the opportunity to learn those lessons."

"Yes," I said, and then told him about the beliefs the early Christian Church held regarding reincarnation.

Bill's understanding of world religions showed promise that this would be a speedy introduction. I went on to explain, "Basically, when we lost our faith and trust and exercised our choice to take control, we separated from God, or from the universal love we call God. This is when we suffered our initial soul loss and left a part of ourselves behind. This initial soul loss preceded all others. Without this first soul loss or disconnection, subsequent soul fragmentation would most likely not have occurred."

"I think I understand, " he said.

"Here, let me draw you a diagram." I got a pad of paper and pen from the table and sketched out the following figure.

Concept of Initial Soul Loss

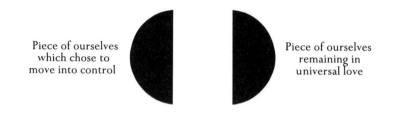

Piece of ourselves
which chose to
move into control

Piece of ourselves
remaining in
universal love

"That makes sense," he said, smiling.

"Great," I said. "Now, let's talk about fear for a moment. Fear is one of the first symptoms of disconnection from universal love and it is what causes soul pieces to detach and break off. So, as we continued our ego-based existence over the millennia, we suffered more and more soul loss."

Turning to a fresh sheet of paper on my notepad, I drew the half-spheres again. But this time, I drew in the concept of continued soul loss.

Concept of Continued Soul Loss

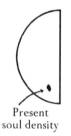

Present
soul density

Piece of ourselves
remaining in universal love

"Within this concept lies the answer to your healing," I said, as I laid the drawing on the table and pointed to the half-circle on the left.

"At this moment in time, as you proceed on your healing path, this is what you may look like in terms of your soul's density. Healing your initial soul loss requires recovering the soul parts you have lost in the millennia since separation. As these lost pieces are recovered, enough soul mass is eventually regained to increase the frequency of your energetic vibrations."

"That's amazing."

"Yes, but what's really more amazing is that once the frequency of vibration reaches a certain level, the two original disparate parts can move into a new state of being, a state of reunification."

"I think I remember something like this from physics," Bill said.

"Yes, this process parallels Quantum Physics' theories governing change of state. When the two pieces are separate, not enough energy exists to unite them. Retrieving lost soul parts adds energy and changes your resonant frequency. As critical mass is attained, the frequency reaches a certain level, and reunification can occur."

"All that just through soul retrieval?"

"Well, it is important to understand that the new healing method I will be giving you, the Gifts as I call them, elevate your frequency in a variety of ways. For example, soul retrieval simultaneously elevates vibrational frequencies while providing a forum for the resolution of core life issues. Furthermore, because you once again have access to the character strengths your lost parts possessed, resolving core life issues becomes ever easier. Once these issues are resolved, the physical and emotional blockages associated with them can be released. As energy begins to flow uninhibited throughout your body, deep healing at a cellular level takes place. This not only heals physical tissue, but also drives your vibrational resonance ever higher. These phenomena, coupled with the opening of your chakras and the enhanced energetic connection you then have with the Universe, leads you to a complete physical, mental and spiritual healing."

"That's really awesome!" Bill exclaimed.

"Yes, literally awesome," I said softly, looking down at my now empty teacup.

"How would you like to take a break and get another cup of tea before we go on?"

"That sounds good," he said. "I think I'll stretch my legs, too. This is a lot to think about."

"Great, I'll see you in a few minutes."

When Bill returned to my office, his face was filled with hope.

"I'm so excited to be moving forward. Total healing would be so incredible. I can't wait to reconnect."

"It is quite a remarkable experience. Please understand, however, that for this reunification to occur, a stable vibrational level is essential. To achieve this energetic stability it is necessary to remain focused and follow through with the entire process. Otherwise your energy levels will spike and fall. Spiking energy levels are not stable enough for permanent reunification and will only provide momentary glimpses of ecstasy."

"I've heard people say they sometimes experience "ecstasy" during meditation when they are overwhelmed by feelings of unconditional love. Is that what you mean?"

"Yes, it is very similar. In meditation, an individual can concentrate their energy, reach out with focus and momentarily touch and be engulfed by universality and unconditional love. With the Gifts, however, when the resonant frequency becomes stable and the two disparate parts reconnect, initial soul loss is healed, and that feeling of love is available to you at all times. To reconnect with that piece, is to reconnect with a part of yourself that is huge and more expansive than anything imaginable. It's like nothing you have ever experienced before. Healing initial soul loss is the ultimate healing. With reunification, you can once again become the inter-dimensional being you were intended to be."

Bill tugged at his chin. "I understand," he said thoughtfully. "It's sort of like reawakening to what life is all about."

"At the very least," I replied smiling.

"Well, I know I want to be healed," he said emphatically. "What do I do now? How do I get started working toward reunification?"

Smiling at his enthusiasm, I replied, "Next week we will begin working with the Gifts. In the meantime, learning to access your intuition would be a very useful tool to support you during the healing process." I then handed him a book I had written called *Tuning In: Opening Your Intuitive Channels.*[2] "Why don't you read over this. It contains exercises and techniques for accessing your intuition through a variety of means, including inner knowing, meditation and dream."

Anxiously, Bill asked, "Do I have to be able to do it all before I can start using the Gifts?"

"No," I said reassuringly, "You don't need to become an expert in accessing intuition or meditation[3] to proceed with the next step. It's just a good idea to have a basic grasp of the concepts and some fundamental ways to apply them. Put simply, intuition involves learning to tune in to the Universal En-

---

[2] For more information on accessing intuitive guidance and on *Tuning In: Opening Your Intuitive Channels* see Appendix A.

[3] For more information on meditation see Appendix B.

ergy Field.[4] You can always come back to the exercises later and increase your proficiency while you are working with the Gifts themselves."

"All right," he replied as a relieved smile crossed his face, "That I can do."

---

[4] For more information on the Universal Energy Field see Appendix C.

CLEARING DENIAL

"I've been waiting for this all week," Bill said enthusiastically as he walked into my office.

"Good," I said as I handed him a warm cup of tea. "We are going to begin with the Gifts today. Let me explain what this first level of the Template's images does." I settled myself into a comfortable chair across from Bill and continued. "The first three images clear your major energy centers," I explained. "In doing so, they reconnect your body energetically, and you are able to clear denial."

"Denial? What do you mean? I don't think I'm in denial, or I wouldn't be here."

"Denial in this sense does not refer to denial of a problem. Rather, it refers to an energetic denial of the ability to fully access memories and information. Memories are often located at a cellular level, as well as a subconscious level. This is why massage therapy and hypnosis sometimes bring to consciousness otherwise inaccessible memories. By implementing the first level of images, energetic pathways are opened and memories are accessed which are instrumental in guiding you forward to a deeper understanding of the root of the problem."

"I see," he said uncertainly.

"Here, let me show you how it works." Using Synergistic Applied Kinesiology[5] I proceeded to assess the flow of energy through Bill's chakras and thymus reflex point. All were shut down.

We sat back down and I handed Bill a chart showing the relationship of each chakra to the health of various internal organs.

"Do you mean that my recurring bronchitis and sinusitis may be in part due to an energetic shutdown?" he asked.

"Absolutely," I replied. "But, don't worry, after you work with these images, your chakras will be reopened and healing can begin. This chart will give you introductory information so you can better understand how you have been functioning."

"I can't believe I never knew this. Do you have more information for me to take home?"

"Here, why don't you read this," I said reaching for another book I'd written entitled *Perceiving Energy: Beyond the Physical Form*. "This book is based on seminars I've taught about perceiving the Human Energy Field[6], as well as other energies

---

[5] For more information on Synergistic Applied Kinesiology see Appendix E.

[6] For more information on the Human Energy Field, energetic shutdown and chakras please see Appendix D.

108

that surround you. It will also help you understand more about how energetic shutdowns can affect your health. In the meantime, let's concentrate on moving forward in your healing."

"What do you want me to do?" Bill asked.

Placing the first set of images on the table for Bill to see, I answered, "I'd like you to look at these images, starting at the right and moving across the page to the left. After you have studied them for a moment, I would like you to sketch them on this piece of paper. Be sure to also sketch them from right to left."

Bill slowly studied the images. A smile came over his face as one image in particular held his attention. "It's as if I've seen this one before," he said pointing to the middle one.

"Yes, that's normal," I replied. "The counterparts to these images are within you, an encoding of sorts. These are merely the tools for unlocking them. Go ahead and finish drawing the images and we will retest your chakras."

As Bill finished, he smiled and said, "I'm done."

"All right, let's stand up and reassess your energy flow." To Bill's astonishment, he now tested open on all major chakras, as well as his thymus reflex point.

"How does that work?" he exclaimed. "I just can't believe it. It's so fast. I didn't feel anything."

"Well, you are lucky," I replied. "Often I have clients who have so thoroughly suppressed their feelings, that when they clear their shutdowns they become dizzy and have to lie down for a while. It's a little like uncorking a bottle of champagne. The gushing forth of energy through a chakra that has been tightly closed can be quite a sensation. After a few moments of rest, the energy flow balances again and things stabilize. For this reason I always tell people to work with the images only when they are at home or a place where they can rest afterwards. Never work with the images while driving a car, for example."

"I had no idea. I'll be sure to take your advice and work with them at home. But how will I know how often to use them?"

"Trust your intuition," I replied.

"What exactly do you mean?" he asked. "I haven't had a chance to start working with the exercises in *Tuning In* yet."

"Basically, in a nutshell, it's trusting your inner voice," I replied.

"Well, how do I know it's not my ego doing the talking?"

"That gets easier with practice," I said reassuringly. "But generally speaking, your ego is the voice which rationalizes and wants to argue back and forth with your inner voice. Your ego is almost always driven by fear. Your intuition, on the other hand, is based on faith, trust and inner knowing."

"I think I understand," he said. "You mean I'll just know when to do them."

"That's right. You'll know when and how often to look at them. Listen to your intuition. Besides, as you work with the images and your energy field opens, your intuition will become naturally stronger and better able to access universal energy."

"All right, I'm going to go home and do those exercises now. I saw there were even exercises for accessing intuition through meditation and dreams in that book. Hopefully I'll get to work on those, too."

"Sounds like you're ready to learn everything at once," I said laughing.

"Well, I'm really ready to move forward," Bill said. "I've been stuck long enough. So, what happens next?" he asked.

Glancing at the clock, I realized that we were out of time. "Well, for today, our session is over. I would like you to continue working with the Level One Images by studying them, sketching them, coloring them and even closing your eyes and visualizing them. You will notice that through this newfound connection you will begin to have remembrances that will take you forward in your healing. Let's discuss those when you are back in town next week. In the meantime, keep a journal to help you process what comes up."

"Sounds great," he said. We shook hands and he headed out the door.

Two days later, I received the following e-mail:

>*Dear Dawn: I just had to write. These images are amazing! So much has happened. All day yesterday, I noticed my internal dialogue kept returning to specific events and situations in my life. I had flashes of having to wash out my own dirty diapers in the toilet. I was so small and it made me feel so ashamed. I also had memories of being beaten and humiliated for wetting the bed. I believe all these experiences added to my feelings of guilt with regard to the genital area. By this morning, I had worked with the images several times and even colored them, when a major realization came to me.*

I had had an argument with my wife over something I needed her to do for the family. As often is the case, she didn't get it done. But, more importantly, a series of excuses was given. I began to realize that I was always giving and when I needed to receive something in return, it was not to be. I then realized that my needs were not being met by my wife, my family, my friends, and especially not by myself. Basically, I was giving everyone around me my time, energy and, most of all, my love, yet I wasn't receiving back. At first,

I couldn't understand why or how people could be so blind. But then I wondered if it was me who was the "blind one?" Had I done something to not deserve their love, respect and support? Hadn't I always been there for them?

Startled at the depth of my frustration, I noticed that for the first time I could clearly see what was wrong. I was connected enough to finally realize I wasn't being loved by anyone, including myself. It is a little scary to realize how deep this runs, yet it gives me hope that I can now actually begin to work on the problem.

Bill's realizations were characteristic of what occurs for many as they clear and open their energy centers. Suddenly they become aware of blockages and shutdowns. In this way they are able to move forward. I encouraged Bill to journal daily and to continue to work with the images as his intuition guided him until our next visit.

❋

Level One Images are most powerful tools, true Gifts. By clearing denial and re-establishing energy flow through our bodies, these images act as keys unlocking our ability to hear how to move forward, as well as reconnecting us with a sense of purpose and desire to heal. Only in cases where someone is severely medicated with anti-depressants or anti-psychotics, or where drug or alcohol levels are high, have I ever seen a sluggish clearing. High levels of such substances in the physical tissue make it more difficult to maintain energetic reconnection for any length of time.

In addition to opening chakras, another remarkable result of Level One Images is the reconnection of energy flow to the thymus. The thymus reflex point, which can be assessed with Synergistic Applied Kinesiology, indicates the strength of your immune system, as well as your will to live, on a cellular and energetic level. Testing energy flow to the thymus reflex point can often provide noteworthy results, as seen in the following case study.

Death Wish

Bob was coerced into seeing me by his mother. She was desperately afraid he had a subconscious death wish. Bob was in his early twenties, had a serious drinking problem, was failing in college and participated in a variety of dangerous activities. After his third DWI, losing his driver's license and being sentenced to a month in jail, Bob appeared in my office, cocky and self-assured. Because he didn't come to see me on his own volition, it was difficult to convince him that his reckless behavior could be a problem. Bob was in total denial.

"I don't know why I'm here," he insisted.

"Well," I replied, "your mother is worried about you. She seems to think you have a subconscious death wish."

"That's ridiculous," he retorted. "She worries too much."

"Do you want to live?" I asked him point blank.

"Of course I do," he replied.

"Good. I am glad to hear it."

After thirty minutes of listening to him insist that there was nothing wrong, I asked, "Would you mind if we tested your body to see if your energy field reflects the same thing?"

"Sure, no problem," he said confidently. Standing up, I guided him into position and he held out his arm for Synergistic Applied Kinesiology testing.

After establishing baseline responses, I tested his major chakras and thymus reflex point. Total energetic shutdown was found, reflecting his deep denial.

Looking at me quizzically, he asked, "What does that mean?"

"It means your energy centers are all closed. But, more importantly, it means that your thymus reflex point has no energy flowing through it. This can be reflective of a suppressed immune system response, which can invite disease into your body. Furthermore, it is significant in that it shows a desire to ultimately stop living."

"I don't believe it," he said.

"I understand," I said. "Let's use a different approach to show you what I mean. Do you remember the baseline testing we did earlier?"

"Yes."

"Remember how when you made a true statement about your name, your arm was strong, and I could not pull it down? That's because the information in that true statement is programmed at a cellular level. It has energy within your body and the response is therefore strong and positive."

"What does that have to do with this?"

"Well, I thought maybe we could simply test you on the statement, 'I want to live.' If you truly believe you want to live, you will test strong."

"No problem," he replied.

Once in position, I said, "Please state, 'I want to live'." He made the statement. I tested his energy flow. Again, his arm dropped weakly by his side.

Tears welled up in his eyes. "Does that mean I don't want to live?"

"What it means," I explained, "is that at some time in your life, and perhaps even many times, you suffered enough of an emotional or physical trauma that you shut down energetically. Possibly you even lost a piece of your soul. Because of these experiences you decided, at a deep, cellular level, that you would rather die. In effect, you programmed your body with a will to die. For some people this manifests in addictions or disease. In your case it has manifested in substance abuse and other reckless behaviors."

"I just can't believe it. Can we do it again?" he insisted.

"All right," I responded. Once again the results of both the thymus reflex point and the statement were negative. This sobering test caused Bob to realize he had indeed programmed his body for self-destruction.

"What do we do now?" he asked in despair.

"Why don't we start by clearing your energy centers and re-establishing energy flow throughout your body. That way you will move out of denial and we can talk about what is really troubling you."

"All right," he agreed reluctantly.

Placing the Level One Images before him, I asked Bob to draw the images on the accompanying sheet of paper.

Just as he finished, Bob looked up at me and suddenly began blurting out his anger. It seemed there was much that needed to be healed.

I am happy to report that this young man courageously chose to move forward in his healing and to work through the entire template and its images on his own.

A few months later, when Bob returned from spring break, I had the pleasure of seeing him for a second time. His whole life had turned around. He had direction and purpose and was committed to being sober and taking care of himself.

The most beautiful aspect of his healing was that none of these changes came from external pressure, they originated from within.

❖

Level One Images facilitate the opening and clearing of the nine major chakras, as well as a number of minor chakras. Traditionally, people have had to practice yoga or meditation for years to achieve the opening of the body's energy centers. Now, with the use of these Gifts, it can be accomplished in seconds. Please understand, these images are not intended to replace yoga or mediation, both of which have many excellent benefits.

The images' ability to clear and open the chakras is due in part to the transcendental nature of the universal energy they emit. This energy vibrationally surpasses individual chakra-based energies and, therefore, assists in clearing the chakra vortexes themselves. This opening and reconnection of energy meridians tremendously activates attunement to your intuitive knowing and exponentially increases your ability to connect with universal energy.

Level One Images can be also be implemented for a variety of additional purposes. For example, when you are ill they can be utilized to open energy blockages and restore an optimum flow of energy to your physical tissue. By reconnecting energy flow to the thymus, the effectiveness of your immune system is enhanced, thereby speeding recovery. Blockages associated with stress or minor setbacks in life can also be easily remedied, often resulting in mood improvement and an increased sense of inner peace.

Before proceeding with the image work itself, it is beneficial to take a moment to assess your present state of well-being and awareness. Answering the assessment questions on the following page will aid you in this process and allow you to more clearly contrast your present state with the state you will achieve while working with the Gifts.

Assessment Questions

Please write your answers to the following questions, being sure to save your answers for later comparison.

1. What brings me joy in life?

2. What do I want to change in my life?

3. What is stopping me from moving forward?

4. What do I want to change about myself?

5. What incidents in my life may have caused me to have energetic shutdown?

6. To move forward in my life, whom do I need to forgive and release anger toward?

7. What are my core issues? How have they repeated themselves in my life?

8. How do I feel about my overall ability to move forward and heal my core issues?

Template of Soul Images – Level One

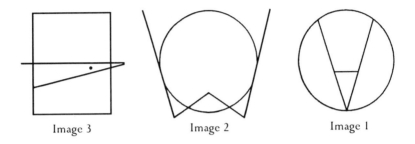

Image 3   Image 2   Image 1

Exercises for Level One Images

1. Copy the images from *right to left*. *Please note: Always read and draw the images from *RIGHT TO LEFT*, as the Template is written in ancient form. The images do not have to be drawn perfectly, however, it is important to arrange them as shown on a single sheet of white, unlined paper.

2. Verbally describe what you have drawn.

3. Trace the images from *right to left* and then color them with whatever colors you are drawn to. I strongly recommend purchasing a box of crayons or pencils with a large selection of colors including gold and silver, because as your vibrational level elevates, you will be drawn to higher vibrational colors.

4. Study the images, one by one, from *right to left*. After each image, close your eyes and visualize the image be-

fore you. They often become three-dimensional during visualization. This is because your higher self is able to perceive the images at a more complex level than your optic nerve can. Visualize the image until its intensity begins to dissipate.

5. Sit back and look at the images. Which one do you like best? Why? This exercise gets you to look at the images in a comparative way. You may find one image more attractive than another. Be sure to follow your intuition.

6. Allow your intuition to guide you as to how often to repeat the process.

After completing the exercises, close your eyes and allow yourself a few moments to center. Now, with this newfound energetic connection, take a moment to once again answer the assessment questions.

Assessment Questions

1. What brings me joy in life?

2. What do I want to change in my life?

3. What is stopping me from moving forward?

4. What do I want to change about myself?

5. What incidents in my life may have caused me to have energetic shutdown?

6. Who do I need to forgive and release anger with in order to move forward?

7. What are my core issues? How have they repeated themselves in my life?

8. How do I feel about my overall ability to move forward and heal my core issues?

Compare the new answers with the original answers you gave before you were cleared. How has increased energy flow affected your assessment of the situation?

Using a journal to record your thoughts, feelings and emerging memories can be very rewarding. Be especially alert to record the new insights and impressions that will reach your awareness. These new knowings, whether they come in the form of a sudden flash of insight into another person's true motives or in the form of a strong inner urge to avoid a particular situation, are the natural result of reopening your connection to your higher self. This guidance and wisdom have always been available to help us create happy lives filled with abundance, but it is our responsibility, and our choice, whether or not to keep the lines of communication open. Regular use of these first images, particularly following any life experience that evokes anxiety or fear, will ensure that you are better able to access the information and guidance available through universal energy.

Journaling also assists you in more rapidly processing the myriad memories and feelings that often come flooding back during the days following use of the Level One Images. As you will see in Bill's experience, trying to absorb and process a lifetime of suppressed realizations all at once can feel a bit overwhelming.

THE WHOLE SOUL

Chapter 16

Storm clouds were darkening the late afternoon sky when Bill next returned to my office. With two hot teas in hand, we began our session, as wind-blown rain began to pelt the dark surface of the lake outside my office window.

Bill shook his head slowly as he looked at me, nodded toward the window, and said, "I feel a little like the weather out there. Stormy and in turmoil. I've suddenly recognized the things that have brought me to where I am now in my life. So many hurts. So many wrongs. I'm overwhelmed. How do I begin to move forward?"

"Where you are is perfect," I assured him. "You are fully connected to all that you have stored in your body. Trust that

123

your experiences occurred for a reason. But, it is no longer necessary to figure out all the reasons "why." Instead, let's continue to move forward and advance into more adventurous territory."

"I'm ready," said Bill.

"Great," I replied. "This next group of images we are going to work with produces intense energetic effects, and provides the gift of soul recovery. Do you remember the first time we visited when we talked about soul loss?"

"Yes," Bill replied.

"Well, in the past you would have had to employ a shaman to retrieve lost soul parts. With the Level Two Images, you are now empowered to heal yourself."

"You're kidding! You mean I can do my own soul retrievals? How about having to learn to journey and all those other things I've read about?"

"None of that is necessary. This is the new way. It's easy, safe, more effective and incredibly quick. What's more, traditional shamanism typically only retrieves present life soul pieces of significant mass. Level Two Images, on the other hand, act like a sieve moving through time. They retrieve lost soul parts from past, as well as present, lifetimes. Even tiny soul fragments of small density do not escape this recovery process."

"That's incredible! I thought opening my energy centers and reconnecting to my inner guidance was pretty impressive, but this sounds like a miracle. How do I do it?"

"Let me explain how the process works. When I observe someone working with Level Two Images, what I generally see is a significant increase in the size of their aura. The periphery of their energy body becomes highly erratic. Then, almost immediately, present and past life soul pieces begin to enter the

124

right side of their energy field. The soul pieces usually appear as light colored shadows of differing energetic densities."

"You mean you can see all that?"

"Yes, I have been able to see energy fields my whole life."

"I really wish I could do that," Bill replied.

"Everybody has the ability to do it," I assured him. "It requires strengthening your optic nerve and increasing your perceptual abilities. The exercises in the book I gave you called *Perceiving Energy* will teach you how to do that and more. But for now, let's stay focused here."

"All right," Bill replied. "How many pieces will I bring back each time I use these symbols?"

"That is a very good question," I said. "The number of pieces you recover with the images varies. Sometimes it may be just a few, other times it could be hundreds at a time. Another important aspect to understand is that there is a tendency for Level Two Images to simultaneously recover past life pieces mirroring the same core issues as the present life pieces retrieved."

"I'm not sure I understand," Bill said.

"Each time you use the second level images, they tend to retrieve soul pieces lost in the same type of trauma. For example, if you retrieve a present life piece who was beaten by his mother, you may also simultaneously retrieve several past life pieces who were similarly abused. The issues that present themselves for healing are often different each time you work with the images. The next time you work with the images, the pieces retrieved then may have been lost during experiences involving something entirely different, such as abandonment or betrayal."

"How can you tell what pieces have returned?" Bill asked.

"Well, one way to verify is to use Synergistic Applied Kinesiology to determine the time, place, and issues surrounding the loss of present life pieces recovered. The circumstances surrounding the past life soul loss could then be investigated by means of hypnosis, meditation or using Synergistic Applied Kinesiology to test intuitive knowing. Past life pieces also frequently communicate through dreams. Either way, a strong correlation can almost always be found between the present and past life issues."

"I had no idea," Bill said thoughtfully. "This sounds like it might actually be possible to heal an issue once and for all."

"Right. Once the pieces surrounding a particular trauma have been retrieved, there is no need to repeat the trauma and your life dramatically begins to improve."

"Well, I'm ready. Let's go get some soul parts!"

Smiling at his enthusiasm, I pulled the first and second level images out of my folder and lay them down on the table. "Why don't you study these for a moment. Remember to read them from right to left, starting at the top."

"No problem," Bill said as he eagerly turned his attention to the images.

"And when you're finished, would you please sketch them here?"

"All right," Bill replied deep in thought.

As I watched him work, I could see the shift occur. Bill began uploading numerous soul pieces. His healing was well underway.

When he finished copying the images, he lay his pencil down, leaned back, looked at me and smiled. "Well, how many pieces do you think I brought back?"

"Let's test you and see," I answered. Using Synergistic Applied Kinesiology to verify results, I found that Bill had retrieved 12 present life soul pieces and 34 past life soul pieces. It was a good start.

As we sat back down, Bill asked, "How do I know what happened to these pieces, when they were lost, why and how?"

"Those are all good questions," I responded, "and we could test each piece further for that information, getting as specific as the day it was lost and the circumstances under which it occurred. This approach takes a long time though. Wouldn't you rather just move forward?"

"Absolutely," Bill agreed. "I've talked myself hoarse in therapy trying to figure out "why." I just want to be healed. But still, it would be interesting to know how I lost them in the first place."

"What you need to know from these pieces will come forward to you in thought, flashback, dream or visualization. In addition to achieving soul retrieval, these images further activate your third eye. This allows you to "see" better, and because you are now connected with universal energy, you will "hear" better as well."

"I understand," Bill said.

"In the meantime, I should tell you that it is not uncommon to be sleepy after soul retrieval or to have food cravings. Please take care of your body's needs and desires. After soul recovery, and prior to integration, people also occasionally notice a mild sense of disorientation. Symptoms have included walking into furniture, and temporary amazement with the modern aspects of life, such as cars, refrigerators, and grocery stores. Some people report that for a day or two it is difficult to remember little things like what day trash pick-up is, or where keys are kept. I even had one client who temporarily couldn't give change at a convenience store because she didn't recognize U.S. currency. During the first few days, flashbacks of old events or traumas are also common. You may even find old thought patterns running though your mind, such as poverty consciousness, unrealistic fears or ideas reflective of a different time period. Don't be alarmed during this integration period. Be patient with yourself. These outdated thoughts reflect the memories and feelings of your recovered soul pieces, and they will fade."

"No problem, my flight doesn't leave until tomorrow morning. I can go straight to my hotel room to journal and rest."

"Great," I said. "And remember, when memories do come to you, the quickest way to reintegrate the soul pieces is through forgiveness." I handed Bill instructions outlining a seven-step forgiveness visualization which facilitates the integration process.

I also gave him the Level Three Images to work with until we met again. "These images provide the gift of integration and greatly accelerate forgiveness," I explained. "Let's keep in touch over the next few days, so I can monitor your progress."

"Looking forward to it," Bill said as he carefully placed the images under his jacket to protect them from the storm.

※

In addition to recovering lost soul pieces, Level Two Images also energize and activate the sixth chakra or "third eye." This energy center, when awakened, enables us to intuit or "see" better. With our third eye activated, information comes to us easily through meditation, dreams, visual images or a sense of certain knowing. These increased perceptual abilities not only provide a forum for recovered soul pieces to present healing information to us, they also strengthen our intuitive and meditative abilities.

From this point forward, it is imperative to be aware of intent when working with the images from the Template of Soul. We always have a subconscious intent, but because we may not be aware of what our subconscious intent truly is, thoughtfully deciding upon and stating our intent deliberately and consciously can be a most powerful tool. For healing through the Gifts, the best intent is an open release to God or the Universe for your highest good.

By releasing your control over the process, the Universe is free to determine the order of soul retrieval that will best facilitate your healing. For example, you may wish to heal issues regarding money in your life. Your ego may lead you to believe that in order to do this, you need to retrieve pieces you have lost specifically related to money issues. In reality, however, since money issues are directly tied to our perceptions about love, it may actually be in your highest good to first retrieve soul pieces related to love. In this way, the core issue underlying the outer manifestation is healed. Once a core issue has been healed, the other situations we have manifested in our lives as symptoms of the core can resolve themselves as well.

If we maintain tight control over the process, however, we limit God's ability to step in and guide us. Here is an example of how to openly release your work:

God, I release this healing work to you, for my highest good.

If you wish to target a specific area, such as retrieving pieces that will help you overcome phobias or some other specific issue, you may wish to try the following method:

1. Hold your specific intention in your mind momentarily:
   My intent is to heal my phobia about heights.

2. Then consciously release it:
   God, I release this healing work to you, for my highest good.

Once you have released your work to God or the Universe, you can trust that the soul pieces you recover and all that you experience are truly for your highest good.

Be open-minded. Remember to check the ego. If you hear yourself saying, "I'll heal this issue first, so I can then access this weakness, and when that is healed I'll be ready for . . .," this is a good indication that your ego is hard at work trying to control the process. Remember that while your ego certainly wants "the best" for you, it simply doesn't know what that "best" really is. Many issues can be healed at once. Often they are linked by a central theme, such as a need for love or ultimately the need to learn self-love.

❋

True to his promise to keep in touch, Bill sent me an e-mail soon after our session:

>*Dear Dawn: After I got back to my hotel room, I felt a rush of memories flooding in and out of my mind. I lay down to rest. Visual images quickly appeared. I remembered a diving accident from a high cliff, yet it was not from this life-time. I was a Polynesian tribesman about five hundred years ago. Apparently I hit the water wrong, broke my back and drowned. I thought how this feeling corresponded to the exact locations in my back where I have been experiencing pain in this life and how I have been unable to find relief. I have gone from chiropractor to chiropractor. The drowning also corresponds to my inability to take deep breaths.*

Another visual I had was of an Indian tribe sitting around a fire. As I walked away from the fire, one of the tribesmen threw a tomahawk at me. I was struck in the back. The feeling of betrayal was overwhelming. I felt I had known that tribesman well. For the next several hours I had a lot of physical pain in these specific areas. I also saw a correlation between the attack from behind and a recent betrayal from my wife and my sister. Over the next few days, I began to recognize all the anger I had been suppressing toward my wife and sister. I also started to see that I felt angry with myself as well, for not honoring myself and loving myself, and for not stopping these people from hurting me. Isn't it interesting that my back now feels better than it has in years?

Bill had been working with the intent to clear his herpes, but had released his work to the Universe. As a result, Bill was able to retrieve those pieces which could lead him to healing the core issues underlying the physical manifestation of herpes. I encouraged Bill to continue working with the Level Two Images. I assured him that his intuition would guide him to know when he was finished. I also explained that he might be drawn to come back and work with the images again, perhaps weeks or even months after completing his initial work with the entire template.

A few days later I received another e-mail from Bill:

>Dear Dawn: In meditation this morning, I was suddenly filled with the strong sense that I was conceived out of wedlock. I decided to investigate this knowing. I went to some relatives I felt I could trust to tell me the truth and discovered my suspicions were correct. My father felt obligated to marry my mother, but never truly wanted to start a family. I'm going to try to find my mother again.

I surmised his mother must have suffered guilt for getting pregnant and unintentionally guilt over to Bill in utero. So often in utero, infants absorb their mother's energetic vibrations and assimilate them as their own.

Additionally, his mother's abandonment of him at one year of age created feelings of unworthiness. Children who have been abandoned or neglected often internalize that the reason for their abandonment or neglect was that they were unworthy of their mother's love. In their minds, had they been worthy of love, their mothers would have stayed and cared for them. Ultimately, these children deny themselves self-love and often become self-abusive. In the end, not only did Bill's mother betray him, but by denying love to himself, he betrayed himself as well.

In an attempt to understand his feelings, Bill began writing letters to anyone who may have known his mother. Unfortunately, a few weeks later, the sad news came. She had died of AIDS two years earlier while working abroad. Bill was never to know his mother.

When we talked next, I explained that sexually transmitted diseases, such as AIDS and herpes, were the physical manifestations of sexual guilt and feelings of being tarnished or dirty. I recommended he reference Louise Hay's book, *Heal Your Body*, in which she states the emotional-mental causes of venereal disease are correlated to ". . . sexual guilt and the need for punishment, public shame, and belief that the genitals are sinful or dirty."

Bill had apparently absorbed his mother's sexual guilt, as well as her shame and feelings of dirtiness. These feelings, coupled with the severe punishment he received for bedwetting, caused him to reject his genitals, regarding them as a source of shame and guilt. His homosexual experience further compounded his sexual guilt. Due to his correlating belief in a need for punishment with regard to the genital area, it was not surprising that Bill manifested herpes. Given this history, it was also not surprising to discover that his mother died of AIDS. Upon further research, Bill later learned that his mother had remarried and that her husband never contracted the AIDS virus himself.

The memories, feelings and knowings that Bill received following his work with the Level Two Images are typical. He chose to investigate further and discovered interesting information that explained many aspects of his core issues. It is important to note that while further investigation and cognitive understanding can be interesting and illuminating, it is not necessary for healing to occur.

Now it is time for you to experience the Level Two Images for yourself.

First, before proceeding with the actual image work:

1. Write your intent.

2. Write your release.

Now, proceed with Level Two Image work.

Template of Soul Images – Level Two

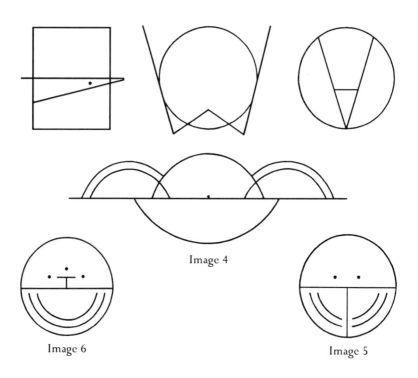

Image 4

Image 6

Image 5

Exercises for Level Two Images

1. Begin by studying image four. One client, a nationally recognized yoga master, became so entranced with this image, he offered the following interpretation. Your interpretation, of course, may vary.

    Image four simultaneously activates energy patterns that transcend past, present and future aspects of time. The horizontal line represents the division between the conscious and unconscious mind, while the three half-circles on top of the horizontal line correlate to past, present and future energies. The outer circles on top of the right and left half-circles help establish auric boundaries to prevent others from seeing in your aura, even though you are aware and connected. The lower half-circle links all three states, and the dot on the line is symbolic of the integration of past and future into present.

2. Now, look at images one through six as shown. Please remember it is important to read and draw the images from *right to left*, starting at the top.

3. Copy the images from *right to left*, starting at the top. While the images do not need to reproduced perfectly, it is important to draw them as shown on a single sheet of unlined, white paper.

4. Verbally describe what you have drawn.

5. Trace the images from *right to left*, starting at the top, and then color them.

6. Study the images, one by one, from *right to left*, starting at the top. After each image, close your eyes and visual-

ize the image before you. They often become three-dimensional during visualization, because your higher self is able to perceive the images at a more complex level than your optic nerve. Visualize the image until its intensity begins to dissipate.

7. Visually review the images. Which one do you like best?

8. Allow your intuition to guide you as to how often to repeat the process.

You may find it useful to journal or meditate after using these images. Again, it is common to feel somewhat disoriented after Level Two Image work. If you feel sleepy, lay down and take a nap. Take time to allow the energy to stabilize. Sleepiness, along with food cravings, is a normal post soul recovery response.

The potential for soul recovery using Level Two Images is enormous. Soul mass increases with each soul piece recovered. As you continue to work with the Gifts over time, the recovery process harmonizes and ultimately balances your *yin* and *yang* energies by synthesizing the male and female aspects of your energy.

Once lost soul pieces have been recovered, the key to moving forward in your healing process lies in reintegrating them into your being. This process begins immediately after recovery and is further facilitated by Level Three Images. Many people find that common post soul recovery symptoms are minimized, if not completely eliminated, by moving immediately into level three integration work.

THE INTEGRATION BEGINS

*T*he soul pieces you have just retrieved must be integrated for healing to be complete. Traditional soul retrieval, and the subsequent reintegration of the retrieved pieces back into our soul mass, once required a great deal of time and conscious integration work. Now, using the Gifts, soul retrieval and the integration process can occur in moments. However, effects such as an increased need for sleep may remain while cellular reprogramming and healing take place.

Integration requires understanding, forgiveness and the release of core life issues on a cellular level. The Level Three Images subconsciously facilitate forgiveness and release, while simultaneously functioning in unison at a cellular level to clear

137

blockages associated with energetic shutdown due to physical or emotional trauma. With the clearing and releasing of blockages, a permanent shift in vibration occurs. When stability at this new, higher level of vibration is achieved, transformational, spiritual and physical healing begin to occur.

As we begin to love ourselves, an evolution in self-actualization occurs. Through this empowerment, profound healing becomes a reality. And as we heal ourselves, a ripple effect takes place. Others see the change in us and begin to walk forward on their own. We thus become an inspiration, a guide.

Template of Soul Images – Level Three

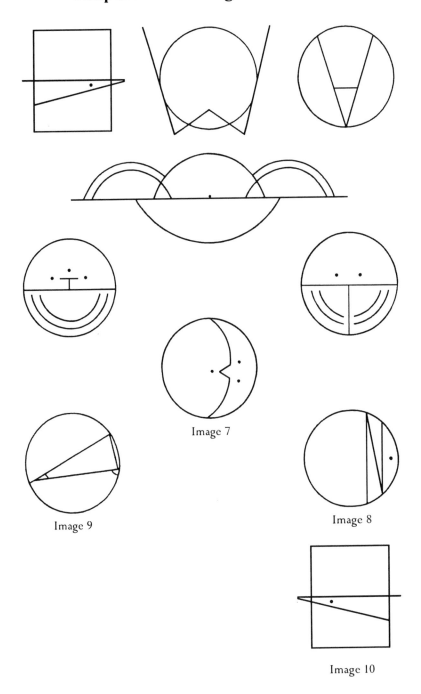

Image 7

Image 9

Image 8

Image 10

Exercises for Level Three Images

1. Look at images one through ten as shown. Draw the images from *right to left*, starting at the top. The images do not need to be reproduced perfectly, but it is important for them to be drawn in the format shown on a single sheet of white, unlined paper.

2. Verbally describe what you have drawn.

3. Trace images one through ten, and color them with colors you are attracted to. Notice how these colors may have changed from the first time.

4. Study the images, one by one, from *right to left*, starting at the top. After each image, close your eyes and visualize the image before you. They often become three-dimensional during visualization, because your higher self is able to perceive the images at a more complex level than your optic nerve. Visualize the image until its intensity begins to dissipate.

5. Visually review the images. Which one do you like best?

6. Allow your intuition to guide you as to how often to repeat the process.

Level Three Images facilitate inter-dimensional connectedness. By reconnecting at this level, you become able to tune into and draw from inter-dimensional nonlinear information, ultimately leading to a cognizant awareness that you are bigger than your present state of being. From this state of awareness, you will be able to look at your core life issues more from a universal point of view. Forgiveness, understanding, and the release of anger, guilt, and regret are then easily achieved at the subconscious level.

Furthermore, by ushering in truth without language, Level Three Images facilitate entrance into a quiet space of conceptual thought, devoid of limiting linear verbiage. Inner peace becomes a reality; and in this quiet state of mind, universal love and acceptance for others come naturally.

Bill reported the following experience to me while working with the Level Three Images:

>*Dear Dawn: During the integration process, I had a difficult time falling asleep because so much was going on. I was filled with a sense of anxiousness. As I visualized the Level Three Images, I felt white and gold light descending upon me, working on me. Then, it felt as though enormous amounts of energy were running through my temples, opening and expanding something inside. It was an incredible experience. I feel so much more alive, calm and at peace.*

It is useful to remember that the disorientation, confusion, strange memories, food cravings or other unusual feelings you may experience during the integration phase, spring from the memories, preferences and personality characteristics of your recently retrieved soul pieces. Level Three Images exponentially accelerate the forgiveness and integration process at a sub-conscious level.

Some soul pieces, particularly those that were lost during extremely traumatic incidents, may also bring their experiences to your awareness through dreams, meditation or images that flash through your mind. When these traumatic incidents are brought to conscious awareness, implementing the following seven-step forgiveness process, in addition to the Level Three Images, further facilitates the integration and healing process.

Remember, too, that we sometimes recover pieces from lifetimes where we may have brought harm to others. In these situations, it is ourselves we need to forgive. We must not live in fear and shame about our past actions. Forgiveness is the key. We must forgive ourselves, and learn to truly love ourselves, as God has always loved us. In this way, we can walk forward in universal love, light, faith and trust.

Forgiveness Visualization

Begin by sitting in a comfortable chair, or lying down. Close your eyes, take a few deep, cleansing breaths and quiet your mind. Now, proceed through the following seven-step forgiveness visualization. If you are currently unable to visualize, simply move through the process on a conscious thought level.

1. **Be aware of what happened**. Visualize the incident. Consciously recognize the details of the experience, whether in this or a past life.

2. **Understand.** Understand why the event occurred from a universal point of view. This can often be the most challenging part of release. For example, we must be willing to admit that people repeat cycles of abuse in an effort to heal. If you were abused, you must recognize that your perpetrator was most likely repeating the cycle of abuse in an attempt to remember and heal the abuse he suffered himself. Or, if your mother did not

meet your needs as a child, it is likely that her needs were not met as a child, and she simply did not know how to meet your needs.

3. **Forgive.** Visualize the person or persons you need to forgive standing before you. Forgive them for what they did and identify how you felt at the time of the incident. For example, if you flash back to your whole family or other loved ones being tortured or killed during wartime, identify your feelings, such as anger, guilt or fear. Then move into understanding that it was a time of war and forgive. You must forgive the person or persons who perpetrated the harm in order to move on.

4. **Let go.** Release the anger, guilt or regret that you hold. Anger is usually a secondary emotion, so look deeper for the boundary that was crossed to make you angry, re-establish the boundary mentally and then release the anger.

5. **Accept.** Move into an acceptance of others just as they are. People cannot always give what we want them to give. This often means we have to let go of our quest for an ideal mother or father and accept that we will never have what we were looking for. And, sometimes we must understand that people are mentally ill and therefore cannot be held to the same standards. Accept others as they are. The only person you can expect to change is yourself.

6. **Surround the person with unconditional love and acceptance.** This means to love them from a universal point of view. It does not mean you have to welcome

them back in your life. Safe boundaries should still be drawn. It simply means to love and accept them, as they are, wherever they are in their healing process.

7. **Announce your intention to live a life filled with love, peace and joy to the person you are forgiving.** Construct statements such as: I only allow people who love and respect me into my life; I believe in myself; I always set safe boundaries; I am healthy; I am filled with inner peace and joy; and I love myself as I am. Be sure to direct these statements to the person you are forgiving. Feel the emotion beneath your words as you say them. Please note it is important to construct only positive statements, being sure to omit negative words such as "not", "no", or "never".

For those who have experienced great pain in a traumatic event, using this formal forgiveness exercise can be of great assistance. Many people are afraid to forgive and let go, because it cuts the ties of anger which hold them locked in certain relationships. Be brave. Practicing forgiveness allows you to heal more rapidly and with greater ease because it expedites the integration of retrieved soul pieces while subconsciously internalizing the forgiveness process.

❂

Maria, a talented young musician, came to me with progressive scoliosis so advanced that she was nearing the point of needing surgery. She had been raised in a home with a physically and verbally abusive father, a background quite characteristic of scoliosis patients. She was extremely shy due in part to the abuse she had suffered, and this was severely limiting her career opportunities. We began her therapy by doing initial forgiveness work related to her father and then proceeded directly to working with the images. The next morning after working with the soul recovery images she e-mailed me this message:

>Dear Dawn: After we finished working with the Level Two Images, I was shocked to learn about the soul pieces that I needed to integrate! Last night, just as I was just beginning to fall asleep, I saw myself as a young girl in a previous lifetime, one in which my present father had raped and murdered me. I "saw" her short life and then told her that she needed to forgive him for what he had done to her. She became quite upset and cried, "But I was RAPED!!! Don't you understand he KILLED me!" She then showed me in graphic detail exactly what he'd done to her and how. Shaken, I got up and went downstairs to reread the forgiveness process from your book. I worked through each step to help her understand and forgive.

When I finished the forgiveness visualization, I returned to bed and began to meditate. I then saw myself as a very young Tibetan boy whose job it was to beat a huge drum all day. He didn't understand why he was doing it, and his drum broke for some reason. Immediately he was filled with terror and confusion. I'm sure this relates to my fear of performing on stage. That is all I was shown. My meditation ended with seeing many people I recognized from school, only they were shown as they looked in different incarnations, not this one.

I'm listening carefully to my inner guidance and am most grateful as I realize the importance of these visuals and how they relate to my overall healing.

I'm happy to report that Maria continued to work with the Template, and over the course of her therapy her scoliosis reversed. Her physical and emotional healing enabled her to overcome the extreme shyness that had crippled her career. She began auditioning nationwide and recently won the privilege of performing at Carnegie Hall.

UNCONDITIONAL LOVE

Chapter 18

Several weeks passed before Bill's schedule brought him back into town. When I finally saw him next, he looked like a new man. There was a spring in his step, strength in his face and a sense of serenity about him that I had not seen before.

"Your work with the Template shows," I told Bill as he settled himself into the chair.

"Dawn, you wouldn't believe the difference working with the images has made," he exclaimed. "Everything is so much clearer now. And I feel so much stronger. I'm taking better care of myself and learning to stand up for myself. Also I've noticed I don't need to be yelling to be heard anymore, because now that I'm respecting myself, other people are respecting me. I feel a confidence I've never felt before which carries over into everything I do. It's wonderful."

"It sounds like you have successfully integrated the strengths and characteristics of your retrieved soul pieces," I said. "The fourth level of images that we will be working with today will continue to elevate and stabilize your vibrational resonance. Over and over, as image work is done, your vibration will rise, then stabilize, then rise and stabilize again."

"I wonder if that's why I've sometimes felt so sleepy."

"That's very possible," I replied. "Often as you enter this phase, it's common for your need for sleep to increase. This is due to the cell tissue repair that is being facilitated. At the higher frequencies cell tissue begins to heal and restructure, as cellular reprogramming becomes permanent. The more elevated your vibrational frequency becomes, the less disease is sustainable in your body."

"I see," he said. "It's similar to why children sleep more when they are growing."

"Basically, yes," I said. "Our bodies need us to sleep for massive healing on the physical level to occur. Once the structure of your physical tissue is ready, you are able to hold the higher frequency steady. In this state, you are ready to soar higher. That's where the Level Four Images come in. Through their vibrational resonance, these images further empower you with higher awareness. They assist you in recognizing the purpose of your existence. Knowing it, you can move forward in your life with renewed direction."

"I've heard people talk about having a life purpose, but until recently, I've never thought I had much of one."

"The fourth level of images will help you understand what it is," I said. "But even more, level four allows you to reach out and realize you are a connected part of the Universe. You will recognize that you are a child of God, and in doing so will be able to embrace your inherent creative abilities. By accessing the power of universal energy, these Gifts help you become all of who you are, which is a co-creator with the Universe." Bill stared at me in silence, absorbing the depth of the words I had spoken.

"You're talking about reunification with our Source," he said finally.

"Yes. When working with Level Four Images, it is common for people to report dreams or meditations in which they have experiences with God, Jesus, the Great Spirit, or whatever form they believe their Creator takes. This is all part of the re-unification process."

"I can't wait to begin," he said softly.

Template of Soul Images – Level Four

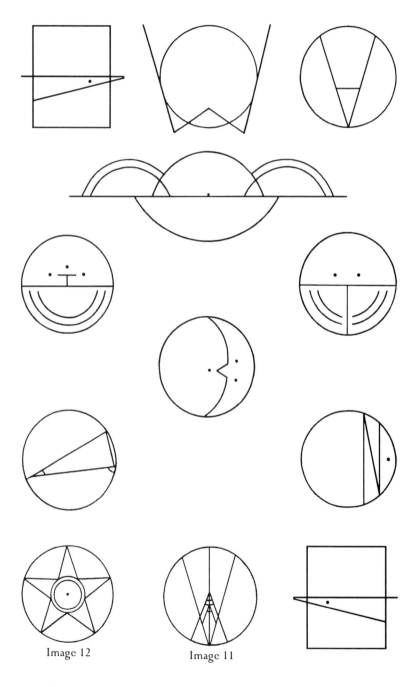

Image 12 Image 11

Exercises for Level Four Images

1. Draw images one through twelve from *right to left*, starting at the top. It is important to draw the images all on one side of a single sheet of white, unlined paper so they appear in the same layout as shown.

2. Verbally describe what you have drawn.

3. Trace and color the images, being sure to use silver and gold if desired.

4. Study the images, one by one, from *right to left*, starting at the top. After each image, close your eyes and visualize the image before you. Continue visualizing the image until its intensity begins to dissipate.

5. Visually review the images. Which is your favorite?

6. Study the images, one by one, from *right to left*, starting at the top. After each image, try vocalizing or singing the image as an alternate exercise. This vocal resonance should be a sound rather than a word. If you are having difficulty, try beginning by singing an "Ohm" or an "Ah" sound at whatever pitch feels right. Let yourself go! Allow the energy to pour forth. Continue singing until you feel you have captured the energetic resonance of the image. Follow your intuition.

7. Allow your intuition to guide you as to how often to repeat the image work.

At this point in the healing process, clients often report truly wondrous experiences. Rapid transformations, both internally and in their external lives, take place. I will share with you Kim's experience:

>Dear Dawn: So many things are happening!!! After this work I feel so much stronger and more comfortable with everything in general. I did want to share with you something incredible that happened last night, but first I must tell you about two other experiences I had. The first occurred a long time ago when I was three years old. I was in a church watching the christening of my newborn sister when I suddenly saw a man with white hair wearing long, light blue robes and a delicate golden crown on his head. He was walking away down a corridor. I tugged at my mother and whispered, "Mom, I just saw God!!!" She told me to be quiet, that I was seeing things.

The event passed and I forgot about Him until I saw the same figure again in a meditation years later. He was helping me in some way, yet never got too close to me, as if He was behind a veil. He felt like a loving, yet distant, grandfatherly figure. The event passed, and I again forgot about Him until last night. Just before I went to sleep, I had been working with the fourth level of the Template of Soul. Later that night I had an extraordinary dream. I found myself in a beautiful place where everyone was in the form of an angel. Everyone was dressed in white and was surrounded by white and gold light. I suddenly had a feeling He was nearby. I asked someone if He was there, and they said He was.

Somehow, the veil, which was like a glass wall that had separated us before, was now gone. He came to me, hugged

*me and said, with tears in His eyes, "I'm so glad you're back."
The emotion was that of a father who hadn't seen his child
from birth and who thought he'd never be reunited with her
again. He felt like the One who had created me in the beginning, transcending all lifetimes. The emotion was completely overpowering, yet gentle, and of pure love. I thanked
God profusely for the experience.*

Bill wrote to me about a similar experience during one of
his meditations after reaching a stabilized level of vibration.

*>Dear Dawn: I appeared in a large crowd of people stand-
ing around a man elevated above us all. I looked at the man.
He held his arms out and welcomed me. At that moment I
felt so loved, I began to cry. Jesus was welcoming me back to
His Kingdom. I felt reunited with God and loved for the first
time in my life. It was after this experience that I realized
God loves us all and doesn't judge us for what we do. We are
the only ones who judge and, therefore, must forgive ourselves. God never left me – I chose to be disconnected.*

*Regarding your message the other day about the prog-
ress of my physical healing, the herpes outbreaks are over. I
had one last minor breakout that was unlike any other I'd
ever had. It felt like the final eruption of old cells and pro-
gramming. It only lasted two days and I wasn't even sore. I
knew intuitively that it was the final release. I'm fully con-
vinced that there will be no further recurrences. I now love
myself unconditionally. I know I no longer need to manifest
any dis-ease to "get" this lesson.*

A few weeks after Bill began working with the fourth level of images, I received an unexpected phone call. "Dawn, I need to come in and see you. Do you have any appointments available for today?"

"Actually, I'm all booked up," I replied. "But, I know you are only here for a little while, so why don't you come in at the end of the day? How does 6:00 p.m. sound?"

"Terrific! I'll be there."

I entered the waiting room to get Bill for his session and could immediately see the look of concern on his face. As we walked down the hall to my office, I asked, "How's everything going?"

"Oh, there's so much going on in my life right now. So many changes. I really need to talk."

"Well, I'm glad you're here. Why don't you go ahead and have a seat. I will get us a cup of tea."

"Thanks," he sighed as he sank down into the leather sofa.

Upon returning, I set the teacups on the table along with a bag of animal cookies from the vending machine. "I thought maybe you'd like a snack, too. You look pretty depleted."

"I am just a little frazzled I think. All this job related travel, along with the restructuring in my company, has made my life a little nerve-racking."

"I understand," I responded.

"Then, on top of that I've been doing the image work and have retrieved several important soul pieces. I have dreams about those lifetimes and get flashes and knowings of what life was like back then. The memory that sticks with me the most though was when I was skewered with a sword. Ever since I had that flashback a few days ago, I can feel exactly where the sword went in. It's right here," he said pointing to the left side of his abdomen.

"Yes, I see," I replied as I looked at the energy in his aura. "What you are feeling is similar to the missing limb phenomenon which amputees experience. You are perceiving the trauma from the past life injury in the recovered soul piece's energy body. Once this piece is integrated and your auric field is balanced and harmonized the sensation will disappear. Have you tried using the Master Image yet to stabilize and help you integrate?"

"No, I haven't gotten that far. I've been so busy."

"I understand. Let's go ahead and do it now."

"Do you think it will help?"

"Absolutely." Reaching into my folder, I pulled out the Master Image and laid it in front of him on the table. "I'd like you to study this image while you slowly turn it counter-clockwise."

As I watched him turn the image, I could see a calmness come over him. He began to smile.

"I feel so much better," he said looking up after he was finished.

"The Master Image reopens your energy centers again. That always helps after a stressful day. Also, you're feeling the result of the harmonizing resonance that helps integrate recovered soul pieces. How does it feel to have the soul piece that was skewered with the sword integrated?"

Reaching down to touch his abdomen, Bill said, "Oh, it's great. And, you're right, the sensation of where the sword went in is all gone."

"I'm glad," I replied. "Please remember to use the Master Image whenever you are experiencing physical sensations from soul recovery or if you wish to speed the integration process. Allow your intuition to guide you when to use it. Now, what else would you like to talk about?"

Bill proceeded to tell me about how he had quit drinking and had drawn safe boundaries with his soon to be ex-wife. At the end of our session, he smiled and said he'd be in touch.

☀

The Master Image contains a micro-system of components previously outlined and holds the power to activate and orchestrate individual images contained within the original template. This multifaceted image serves many purposes, foremost of which is the almost instantaneous integration of recovered soul pieces. No longer does it require days for you and your retrieved soul pieces to adjust to one another's frequencies. After soul recovery you and each of your retrieved soul pieces resonate at unique vibrational frequencies, depending on age, life experiences, emotions, and circumstances surrounding the trauma causing soul loss. Imagine a table upon which a variety of objects are vibrating at different speeds. This is similar to what your energy body is like with a plethora of recovered, but still unintegrated, soul pieces vibrating in it. If the different objects on the table were synchronized and all began to vibrate at a higher resonance, they could be blended or merged into one. This is how the Master Image achieves the reintegration of your soul pieces in only moments. It raises the vibration of your disparate soul pieces, along with your own present vibration, to a new, higher frequency at which you and your pieces can blend and become one. Once integrated, you regain the character strengths that these pieces possessed, along with their insights.

Additionally, the Master Image and its components also stabilize your energy field. This can be most helpful after soul retrieval when people often "feel" injuries where none have been inflicted in this lifetime, a phenomenon similar to the "missing limb" sensations experienced by amputees. For example, if you recovered a past life piece who had had a sword thrust through his abdomen, it would not be uncommon to experience some vague abdominal pain until that soul piece integrated. This pain is the energetic residue of the original damage suffered in the soul piece's energy body. In these instances, the Master Image not only integrates the recovered piece, but also heals the residual etheric damage suffered in the trauma.

Master Image

Exercises for the Master Image

1. Copy the image shown above on a sheet of white, unlined paper.

2. Rotate the sheet of paper counter-clockwise full circle. Stop and study the image during rotation if you are guided to do so. Continue to rotate it until you feel you are done.

The healing properties of the Master Image are profound. This image provides instantaneous integration of recovered soul pieces, while harmonizing the energy field and repairing residual etheric damage from past life injuries. In addition to assisting in the integration process, this image also clears denial and reopens blocked or sluggish chakras, allowing you to once again reconnect with universal knowing and guidance. This image can be useful in your daily life as well. For example, after a trauma or other unpleasant incident, it can help you regain balance, stabilize your energy body, and even repair tears in your aura.

LIVING IN LOVE

W hen I was given the Gifts, I was told it was time to offer the world a quick and efficient way to heal. Healing had to be available to all, to anyone who was ready to choose it.

These Gifts awaken our inherent ability to heal ourselves, and in doing so empower and enable us to create the life we desire. Many people perceive God or the Power of Creation as an external force. In reality, the Power of Creation lies within us all.

Every day of our lives we have the power to create love, happiness, joy and wealth, as well as the sometimes unpleasant situations that aid us in healing our core life issues. Many people, unfortunately, have conditioned themselves to feel helpless. They feel that they have no power to choose how their lives will be. Some even believe they are destined to be unhappy, poor, sad, angry, depressed, guilty, abused or betrayed. Many have resigned themselves to living life without joy, settling for security rather than fulfillment. Living in "happy denial," they cease to aspire wholeness. Believing themselves to be powerless, they remain stuck waiting for something or someone to come along and change their lives.

These Gifts were given to assist us in creating the happy, prosperous lives we were meant to live. A portion of the evolution of soul relates to the healing of soul fragmentation and our connection with universal energy. Another part of that evolutionary process involves elevating the vibrational level of energy reverberating within us to a level where we can utilize all of our inherent gifts, such as extra sensory perception, telepathy, and intuitive guidance. Anyone who chooses to learn, focus their attention and practice, can use their extra sensory perception, gain insight through intuition, heal and find purpose in life. Most of our life problems are caused or exacerbated by not tuning in to our higher selves and listening to the guidance available within.[7]

❋

Each time you work with the template, your vibrational frequency increases as more soul mass is integrated, and the energy blockages associated with the lost pieces' traumas are released. As critical density is approached and stabilization is achieved, the long awaited moment arrives: the spontaneous

---

[7] For more information on accessing your intuitive awareness please see Appendices A, B, C, and D.

reunification with the core soul piece left behind at the time of initial separation. This inter-dimensional reunification with the original part of ourselves, which has remained connected with universal truth, love and light, has profound effects barely describable in the language of our three-dimensional world. Some people describe it as "being born again." This does not reflect a choice to be Christian, but rather the awe-inspiring reunification with that which they were disconnected from so long ago. This reconnection, accompanied by the opening of the cosmic and higher self chakras, ushers in a broadening understanding of universal law.

Those who have experienced this rebirth in reunification report similar experiences, the most common of which is an overwhelming feeling of absolute, complete unconditional love. This blissful experience of love is similar in description to the experience of unconditional God love encountered by those who have had near death experiences.

Bill shared the following insights with me regarding his own revelations.

>*Dear Dawn: I see everything so differently now. All that is connected with love, harmony, and universal truth describes what we call Heaven. It certainly exists on Earth. I no longer consider Heaven a place, but feel it as a state of being. Hell for me is about being disconnected, unbalanced and in denial. In Hell, I walked this Earth in fear, frightened I wasn't good enough, afraid I didn't deserve love, and anxious over dozens of large and small daily matters. Now that I am reconnected, I am in Heaven. I feel the energy and exuberance of being in a body that is free of pain. I feel the joy of being surrounded by love – of God's love for me, of love for myself,*

and of love I feel for others. I feel the peace and safety that comes from knowing that I can handle anything life brings me, because I am connected. Dawn, even if these Gifts had "only" healed my physical body of herpes and put an end to the repetitive emotional patterns I was painfully acting out in my life, I would have been more than thrilled. But to now experience the wonder of reconnection is more than I could ever have imagined. Serenity had just been a word that I'd intellectually understood, but had never before really experienced. All my life I had believed that I had to be "good enough" to someday "get into" Heaven. Now I understand that Heaven isn't someplace we someday go to. Heaven is what we make on Earth right here, right now, when we're connected.

Bill, like so many others, went on to discover that God does not judge. God has never judged. We have been loved unconditionally since the beginning of time. What we deemed "mistakes" were merely learning experiences. With that discovery, we quickly understand that we no longer need to judge others or ourselves. We are filled with universal love and radiate the light of this unconditional love energy out to all.

With reunification, we instantly know that we have always been completely loved by God. Once this realization occurs, total, unconditional self-love becomes possible. As the vibration of pure love fills our bodies, deep, complete physical healing occurs. This shift in the electro-magnetic resonance in our physical cells brings about the release of toxins and blockages held at the cellular level. With physical toxins and energetic blockages released, the psychological and spiritual healing we have set in motion raises our cellular resonance and allows our physical tissue to heal.

As our soul density increases with each soul piece retrieved and integrated, more and more of our core issues are healed. With this healing, old patterns of behavior are left behind, and we begin to interact with people in a new way. We choose to set safe, healthy boundaries regulating our involvement with others. By changing the roles we play in life, our friends, adversaries and family members must change their roles as well.

As we draw safe boundaries and redefine our lives, it is not uncommon to experience a temporary loss of passion or drive for things previously of interest. Have faith, passion resurfaces after your new path has been laid. All the while, you become evermore filled with knowing, peace and joy. Spend time experiencing this serenity as it can provide a great sense of comfort and harmony during this transition period. You are the creator of your future. Feel your connection with the Universe and move forward on your new path with love, faith, and peace.

❂

God has given us a priceless gift; through this Template of Soul, He has given us a way home. However, as in the beginning of time, the element of choice remains with us.

Will these images produce a change in you? Absolutely. But, as with anything, you get out of it what you put into it.

Repetitive core issues that are denied and suppressed are like splinters left under your skin to fester. When you work with these images, they will draw out the festering issues from within, like a splinter that is finally drawn to a head. It is your task to address these issues with the newly gained character strengths of your retrieved soul pieces. With those new strengths and your newly opened channel to guidance, you will have the opportunity to finally remove and heal that which has festered within you for so long. You need never again be solely dependent on others, such as shamans or therapists, for your healing. You now have the keys to heal yourself.

When feelings of fear, anger, frustration or any other emotion that causes discomfort arise, look inward for the cause. Look for what is under that surface emotion, and remember, it is a choice to be angry, fearful or frustrated. No one else can force you to feel that way. By stretching your understanding and practicing forgiveness, you can choose to let go of your anger or fear and move on. When you are at peace and love yourself, you will know the joy of living in love.

When Bill first came to see me, he seemed spiritually aware and open, yet he was in denial. He was disconnected from his higher self and not able to recognize what was wrong. Until he opened himself up by reconnecting and following his path, he could not heal. He did not understand that to find the love he so desperately desired, he first had to love himself, and that could not happen until he believed he was worthy of love. Intellectually understanding these concepts is one thing, but to heal at a cellular and spiritual level, so that permanent change can occur, is quite another. Bill is now ready to be surrounded by people who love and support him. Bill is now ready to love and support himself.

You may choose to heal at any speed you wish. Being a co-creator with God, all you need do is set your intent.

Your new path will unfold before you as you heal and leave old ways behind. No longer will your time and energies be consumed playing out the same old painful patterns in another attempt to learn unlearned lessons. Instead, you will move forward to create a life filled with love.

May you walk a Blessed Path
as you fill your life with Love and Light.

ACCESSING YOUR INTUITION

*E*ach of us possesses the natural gifts of extra sensory perception, telepathic communication and intuitive guidance. These are not special talents given only to a select few, but are inherent within us all. They lie latent within us until we elevate our energetic frequencies to a level where we reopen our energetic lines of communication with our higher selves and universal energy. Fear and denial shut down this connection. Part of the process of soul healing involves reopening that connection to our higher selves.

Many people ask, "What is higher self?" Your higher self resides within you and has the capability of connecting with the Universal Energy Field, thereby accessing universal knowing in order to guide you. Intuition is the knowing received when this higher awareness is accessed. When we refer to a higher self, a lower self is inherently implied. This lower self refers to the disconnected self, the one who lives in fear, allowing the ego to dominate and drive decision making.

Listening to your inner voice and intuitive guidance, as opposed to following the standard or accepted course of action dictated by society, is often necessary to achieve inner healing. This can be difficult for the ego because it may involve facing the unknown.

The ego often reacts with, "Don't go there, we don't know what will happen!" Through statements such as these, which we may be only barely conscious of, the ego convinces us to not move ahead into the unknown by insisting, "We may get hurt." This is when intuitive thought and the ability to connect with universal energy become indispensable.

Intuitive guidance is available to us all through inner knowing, visualization, meditation and dream. Anyone who chooses to, can learn to access their intuitive guidance, communicate telepathically and receive information about this world through their "sixth sense" of extra sensory perception.

Introductory Exercise for Increasing Intuitive Perception

One of the easiest ways to open up to your inner voice is to play a game with yourself by asking your intuition to answer questions like those which follow. Please note that when people become aware of their inner voice, or intuition, most do not actually hear a "voice" speaking to them in their ear or in their head. Information is generally received as a flash of knowing or an idea.

Pay attention to your first impulses. They are usually correct. The later or secondary "voice" tends to be the ego arguing with the intuition.

168

1. Who is calling on the telephone?

2. Has the mail come yet?

3. Which team will win?

4. Do I have e-mail? If so, how many?

5. Which checkout line at the grocery store will move quicker?

6. Will the stock market index rise or fall?

This new capability you are developing is like a muscle that has not been used in a long while. Time and practice are required to build strength and confidence. Positive reinforcement is important. When your inner voice proves to be right, pat yourself on the back and take notice. This acknowledgment helps you become ever more aware of your inner knowing. Keep track of your successes for two weeks and you will be pleasantly surprised to see how quickly your accuracy increases.

More information on accessing your intuition, along with a variety of techniques, exercises and easy step-by-step guidance, is offered in *Tuning In: Opening Your Intuitive Channels.*[8]

---

[8] See other titles by author.

MEDITATION

*T*he ability to meditate is a powerful tool for accessing intuitive guidance. Only by learning to quiet your mind can you "hear" the guidance being offered. Additionally, meditation has proven effective for stress management; lowering cholesterol; improving sleep patterns; easing high blood pressure; manifesting health, happiness and wealth; and in releasing endorphins for an increased sense of well-being.

Meditation can occur in both Alpha and Theta brain wave states. Meditations in Alpha are relaxing and often reflective, but for the novice can initially be characterized by a struggle to quiet the mind. Much intuitive guidance, however, can be accessed at any moment of the day just by taking a few deep breaths, closing your eyes, quieting your mind and shifting to a predominantly Alpha brain wave frequency.

Meditations in Theta differ substantially. In these meditations, it is common to lose consciousness of your body. This means you are simply not aware of your temporal structure at all. Often you enter a place of total silence, serenity and universal love. These meditations are significantly deeper than those experienced in Alpha and can have profound healing potential. When this brain wave pattern is foremost in amplitude, permanent cellular reprogramming and change can occur. Learning how to access Theta can be most beneficial and is optimal to enhance your healing.

More information on this topic, as well as quick, easy methods for facilitating rapid and consistent entry into meditation, is available in the author's work entitled *Tuning In: Opening Your Intuitive Channels.*

THE UNIVERSAL ENERGY FIELD

*T*he Universal Energy Field surrounds us at all times and makes an energetic continuum available for the reception of information and telepathic communication. Intuition manifests in many ways ranging from quiet knowings to strong gut feelings. You may even experience flashes of visuals before your eyes.

Where do knowings like, "She's coming up the driveway," or "I knew it was him calling," come from? The knowing you are experiencing is information picked up through the Universal Energy Field. If someone is projecting a thought or idea, you can easily tune in to this energy projection. The trick is to quiet the mind enough to hear the knowing and honor it.

We access intuitive guidance when we attune to the Universal Energy Field, the energy that connects all things. The concept of a Universal Energy Field has existed for millennia and permeates many cultures. Differing cultures have called this energy by various names. In India, for example, universal energy has been known as *Prana* for over 5,000 years. This force, *Prana*, is believed to permeate all life. Similarly, over 4,000 years ago, the Chinese gave the name of *Chi* to the universal energy believed to surround and compose all matter; *Chi* is believed to be the source of all life.

For more information on how to access intuitive guidance through the Universal Energy Field, perceive energies in nature, or perceive the Human Energy Field, please reference the author's works entitled *Perceiving Energy: Beyond the Physical Form* and *Tuning In: Opening Your Intuitive Channels.*

THE HUMAN ENERGY FIELD

*T*he Human Energy Field or aura is the result of the energy we radiate from our feelings, thoughts and physical being. It can be seen as a bubble of light or color surrounding the body. All of your outer and inner expressions result in a manifestation of light vibration. The Human Energy Field or aura has a direct correlation to a person's emotional, psychological and physiological state. Past emotional trauma or abuse often cause a "shutdown" or cessation of energy flow through certain regions of the body. If these shutdowns are allowed to remain for long periods of time, a physical manifestation of illness usually occurs within the body.

Many people today, as products of the Scientific Age, are reluctant to accept the presence of a Human Energy Field or aura until it is "proven" to them. Unfortunately, until we have experienced it, until we have learned to see it or feel it, we tend to dismiss its very existence. In doing so, we deny ourselves a tremendous healing resource. If you wish to learn how to perceive the Human Energy Field, as well as other energies which surround you, easy step-by-step guidance is offered in *Perceiving Energy: Beyond the Physical Form.*[9]

Chakras

Through the realization that our bodies are structured with atomic particles, which vibrate light, a better understanding of chakras or energy centers can be achieved. It is interesting to note that animals have chakras as well. Energy centers and auric fields are particularly easy to perceive on larger animals such as dogs.

The name chakra is derived from an East Indian word for wheel, and in fact, when these energy centers are open and activated, the energy emitted from them does actually spin like a wheel. Furthermore, when open and activated each chakra projects a flow of vibrating energy through it that creates a color and sound corresponding to its location in the body.

When an energy center is blocked, the light, or energy, which is normally able to pass through it, will be slowed and become gray or dull. Each chakra reflects the energetic health of a particular aspect of our mental-emotional expression. In addition, the amount of energy flowing through each chakra affects specific aspects of our physical bodies.

---

[9] See other titles by this author.

Blockages of energy though the body's chakras and energy meridians diminish our mental, emotional and physical well-being. By re-establishing energy flow, energetic meridians are activated, thereby enabling you to access information contained in physical cell tissue, old memories and etheric information.

The Nine Major Energy Centers

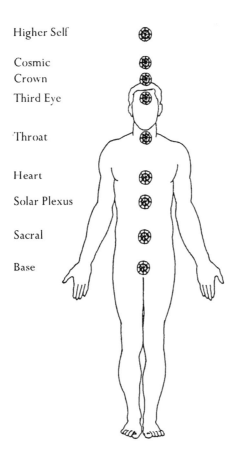

Higher Self

Cosmic
Crown
Third Eye

Throat

Heart

Solar Plexus

Sacral

Base

1. *The Base or Power Chakra* is located at the base of the spine and when open, emanates the color red. This chakra represents sex as well as survival, and pertains to how assertively we seek our goals. Open base chakras dramatically increase capabilities for manifesting.

2. *The Sacral Chakra* lies in the abdominal area just below the navel. It is related to the reproductive system and emanates the color orange when open. This energy center is reflective of a body's vitality and health and relates to overall connection of energy meridians.

3. *The Solar Plexus or Creative Chakra* lies in the upper stomach region or solar plexus, which is located at the soft tissue just under the breastbone. This center is where we get our "gut" feelings from and vibrates with the color yellow. Our thoughts, ideas and will power are reflected in this chakra, and much of our intuitive guidance about other people comes from energetic connections originating in this center.

4. *The Heart Chakra* lies in the middle of the sternum approximately two fingers' width above the bottom of the breastbone. This center is utilized to feel and understand others so that we may live in harmony and balance. This chakra emanates a beautiful green, which can often be seen streaming forth in a magnificent radiance from those who are newly in love. Negative emotions such as vanity, jealousy, guilt, regret and envy can cause the heart chakra to shut down.

5. *The Throat Chakra* is located in the hollow area just below the Adam's Apple and vibrates blue. This center's primary purpose is communication.

6. *The Third Eye Chakra* is located on the forehead in between the eyes and is responsible for visualization and pictures in dreams or meditation. When open, this chakra vibrates violet and can become a powerful tool for telepathy.

7. *The Crown Chakra* lies at the top of head and usually emanates clear or white. Often as one progresses along a healing journey, the crown will begin to open, and the energy sensations associated with the newfound energy flow can feel like tingling or itchy scalp.

8. *The Cosmic Chakra* lies approximately six inches above the crown, represents our link to universal thought and is silver in color. Deeper understanding of basic universal principles, such as karma, abundance, the oneness of everything and reincarnation, is facilitated through this chakra.

9. *The Higher Self Chakra,* located approximately eighteen inches above the crown chakra, is the center of higher enlightenment and provides a great sense of inner peace and knowing. When open, this energy center vibrates gold and provides protection by enabling the transmutation of negative energy.

SYNERGISTIC APPLIED KINESIOLOGY

Appendix E

*A*pplied Kinesiology is a system of muscle testing techniques developed by Chiropractor George Goodhart to obtain information from the body's cellular intelligence. A wide variety of practitioners, including nutritional consultants and chiropractors, employ Applied Kinesiology to assess physical conditions, access the body's intelligence, and identify allergies and nutritional needs.

My practice requires a broad range of techniques to evaluate my clients' conditions, assess energy flow through the chakras, provide a forum for psycho-emotional testing and test core beliefs stored at the cellular level. To meet these needs, I developed a synergistic approach to Applied Kinesiology. This approach provides a clear, concise and concrete method of assessing the Human Energy Field and validating certain other intuitive information.

Synergistic Applied Kinesiology is an effective tool for assessing energy flow through the body and identifying blockages. Having blockages, or even complete shutdowns, in your energy field is common as you begin your healing journey. Many illnesses are in actuality the physical manifestations of energy shutdowns in the Human Energy Field. As energy ceases to flow to certain areas, disease is allowed into the body through the accumulation of toxins and the subconscious suppression of the immune system.

Synergistic Applied Kinesiology can also be used to test and verify the results you obtain with the images. Just as we have different energetic vibrations at different ages in our lives, recovered soul pieces vibrate differently than you do at this moment. Your body and your energy field have an innate awareness of how many new, distinct vibrational energies exist in your field. Because of this differential, Synergistic Applied Kinesiology can be used to ascertain the number of soul pieces recovered during Level Two Image work, or the number of soul pieces integrated during Level Three Image work.

While testing provides validation that a particular chakra is, in fact, open or that a specific number of soul pieces have indeed been recovered, it is not necessary. For most people, the memories, realizations, physical sensations and other direct effects of using the images are proof enough that something quite miraculous is occurring.

This book and other titles by Dawn E. Clark are available through your local bookstore, or if you prefer:

Order by Fax, Phone or by Mail
For your convenience, the order form below may be copied or cut out for fax or mail orders. For fax orders, please include your credit card information. For mail orders, please enclose your check, money order or credit card information.

The Center for New Beginnings
P.O. Box 5485
Kingwood, TX 77325-5485

(281) 359-1069 Fax
(281) 359-5154 Phone
Please have your credit card number available.

Name _____ Phone _____

Address _____
  Street   City   State   Zip

Title	Price	Qty	Total
Gifts for the Soul: A Guided Journey of Discovery, Transformation and Infinite Possibilities	23.00		
The Gifts in Action: An Interactive Guidance Workbook for Gifts for the Soul	13.50		
Tuning In: Opening Your Intuitive Channels	12.95		
Perceiving Energy: Beyond the Physical Form	12.95		
Sub Total			
Less 20% discount for multiple orders			
Shipping and Handling (see below)			
(TX Residents Only) 8.25% Sales Tax			
Total			

Shipping and Handling: 1 book @ 3.95, each additional book add $1.75
All orders shipped within 48 hours of receipt.

Credit Card Number _____

Signature _____ Exp. _____

Throughout the day, whenever you are tempted to be fearful, remind yourself that you can experience LOVE instead.

We all have the power to direct our minds to replace the feelings of being upset, depressed and fearful with the feelings of inner peace. I am tempted to believe that I am upset because of what other people do or because of circumstances and events which seem beyond my control. I may experience being upset as some form of anger, jealousy, resentment or depression. Actually, all of these feelings represent some form of fear that I am experiencing. When I recognize that I always have the choice between being fearful or experiencing Love by extending Love to others, I need no longer be upset for any reason.

BE STILL

Happy - Free - Thoughtful - Kind - Honest - Loving - Mindful - peaceful - fearless - (thankful) for Enlightment - opening of the mind/soul to the Love and Light - Unity with God. - I must listen to my intuition. -

I AM DETERMINED TO SEE THINGS DIFFERENTLY.
Now I recognize that my responses are determined only by the decisions I make. I claim my freedom by exercising the power of my decision to see people and events with Love instead of fear.
Our state of mind is our responsibility. Whether we experience peace or conflict is determined by the choice we make in how we see people and situations, whether we see them as worthy of Love or as justifying our fear. We do not have to act as robots and give others the power to determine whether we will experience Love or fear, happiness or sadness.
Whenever you feel tempted today to see through the eyes of fear, repeat to yourself with determination:
"I am not a robot; I am free.

I am determined to see things differently."

Through out the day when you are tempted to hurt yourself through attack thoughts, say with determination: I WANT TO EXPERIENCE PEACE OF MIND RIGHT NOW. I HAPPILY LET GO ALL ATTACK THOUGHTS AND CHOOSE PEACE INSTEAD.

Loving yourself - fearless   "BE STILL" - Peaceful, happy, focussed - present day living.

P. 99 - it Starts. self-healing- dealing with the present.
Reconnection with oneself. We have a quest to reunite
with God.

P. 101- Initial Soul Loss

P. 167- Accessing your Intuition (Including inner knowing,
meditation, and dream.)

171 - Meditation - intuition involves learning to tune in
to the Universal Energy Field.

173- Universal Energy Field